Ascendant Sign Archetypes

Grace Davison Topping

Member

American Federation of Astrologers

and

The Rosicrucian Fellowship

ISBN: 0-86690-470-0

First Printing: 1998

Published by:
American Federation of Astrologers, Inc.
PO Box 22040
6535 S. Rural Road
Tempe, AZ 85285-2040

Printed in the United States of America

Dedicated to Mary Marguerite Davison

Contents

Introduction

Astrology is ancient, which may be the only safe statement one can make about it. It is such a controversial subject that even astrologers do not agree on how it should be classified. Some refer to astrology as a science and others refer to it as an art. It cannot be placed into any one category for it encompasses a number of categories.

Astrology has been called a good many things down through the ages and has withstood the abuse of many people, but it still prevails and has prevailed since the dawn of history.

The earliest records on astrology came from Mesopotamia in the seventeenth century BC, and it is believed that as early as the fifth century BC, the Babylonians drew up the first zodiac dividing the heavens into twelve equal sections. Cicero, the renowned Roman lawyer and statesman, said, "Nobody can deny to the heavenly bodies the possession of reason unless he himself is destitute of reason."

Astrology has guided mankind for centuries and will continue to do so till the end of time.

An astrology chart has been compared to a road map and it could be considered a road map of the heavens because it is a guide for our journey through life. People refer to road maps when they travel through unfamiliar territory but it is the rare person who will refer to an astrology chart. Many people have not even seen their chart since first embarking on the most important journey of all, their journey through life. In a study of charts on those who had no knowledge of astrology, the significant events that had occurred in their lives could be detected by the activity of the planets or, to use the road map analogy, the significant events stood out like sign posts showing changes taking place on their journey.

We study the migratory behaviour of birds and animals and marvel that these, God's creatures, know when to start their journey and in which direction to travel. Is not man also guided by a Supreme Power? Long before we took our first breath, our soul had chosen which planetary pattern held the lesson it needed for its next evolution and it is here that our journey first begins.

We live the life our soul selects from the heavens in order that we may gather experiences and transmute them into soul growth (Lessons in *The Rosicrucian Fellowship Philosophy*).

Do we have the privilege of free will? Of course we have free will. We have the free will to live up to our highest promise or sink to the lowest ebb that is permitted within the boundaries of our planetary pattern. We are not fated to behave in one way and one way only or to travel down just one path without taking any detours or side trips on our journey. Some souls explore the infinite variety of possibilities in their heavenly mix, while others steadfastly follow life's main highway.

We have the free will to choose what we will make of our trip.

Books have been written using Sun signs alone and some fascinating information can be gleaned by reading your own Sun sign description. The twelve signs of the zodiac describe each person born under the Sun.

It is interesting to note that in ancient times, people so believed in the soundness of these Sun sign characteristics that it became the basis of our modern jury system. In those early days, the courts determined that a jury should consist of twelve men because it was believed that if one man from each of the twelve Sun signs was chosen to sit on a jury, the verdict would be fair and just.

You undoubtedly have met someone with the same Sun sign as you who appeared vastly different than you in personality and appearance. Some individuals have discounted astrology because of this difference. The reason why two people with the same Sun sign can appear so unlike each other is because they have different Ascendant signs.

Your Sun describes your will or ego drive and your Ascendant describes your personality and physical appearance. It shows what picture you put before the world. Make no mistake about it, two people with the same Sun sign will have the same will or ego drive but if their Ascendant signs differ, they will be very unlike each other in personality and appearance.

An Aries with an Aries Ascendant and an Aries with a Cancer Ascendant will appear vastly different from each other but they each will possess the same will to be first or to excel in some area of their lives as expressed by their Aries Sun.

The Ascendant sign is the zodiacal sign rising above the eastern horizon at the time of your birth. It is the key determinator of your chart for it is the basis of your personality and the blueprint of your appearance. Every twenty-four hours the twelve Sun signs travel over the Ascendant, each sign taking approximately two hours to complete its cycle. The time of your birth determines which sign rises on your own personal Ascendant. The twelve signs of the zodiac are constant in their description. That is to say, the basic characteristics described by the sign on your Ascendant will be similar for all individuals having the same Ascendant sign. If you were cast in the mold of an Aries Ascendant, your description would be fundamentally the same as all others possessing an Aries Ascendant. After giving consideration to hereditary, socioeconomic and environmental qualities, this basic similarity will remain unchanged. Planets on the Ascendant can alter the description somewhat but an Aries Ascendant will always provide a proud nature and a ramrod straight posture with a full measure of fast action and impatience.

Your Ascendant sign and the placement of the Sun in your chart bear the same relationship as the Sun in our solar system does to the horizon of planet earth. When it is noon, the Sun is at its highest point in the sky directly overhead. If you were born at noon, the Sun would be on your Midheaven or at the top of your chart; if you were born at midnight, the Sun would be on your Nadir or at the bottom of your chart; if you were born at sunrise, the Sun would be on your Ascendant or rising on the eastern side of your chart; and if you were born at sunset, the Sun would be on your Descendant or setting on the western side of your chart.

The earth's horizon embraces a good deal of irregularities which negates an easy solution for timing the sun's rise on any particular day or place. For this reason, a short table is provided to indicate the approximate time that each sign rises on the Ascendant. These are general timings limited to Northern Hemisphere births. If you require a mathematically precise calculation of your birth chart, you might consider one of the many computer services which provide reasonably priced chart printouts.

The tables herein indicate cut-off dates for each Sun sign. If you are a cuspal birth and the tables list your birth date in the sign previous to your Sun sign, my apologies. Space prohibits the listing of birth dates for each individual year. However this should have no bearing on your Ascendant sign, i.e., if you were born at 8:30 a.m. on June 21 and the Sun had just entered the sign of Cancer, your Ascendant sign would be Leo whether your Sun is in the sign of Cancer or the preceding sign of Gemini.

To find your Ascendant description, turn to that section which holds your Ascendant sign. If you do not know the sign on your Ascendant but you know the time of your birth, use the tables to locate the sign rising at that time. You may run into an intercepted sign which would alter your chart slightly so if you disagree with the description given, read the descriptions for the time of birth immediately before and immediately after your birth time to find the one which best describes you. On rare occasions, an intercepted sign will fall on the Ascendant giving a person two signs on the Ascendant. A client of mine has Pisces on her Ascendant with Aries intercepted and both are evident in her personality.

If you do not know the time of your birth, you may be able to determine your ascending sign by reading all of the Ascendant outlines given for your Sun.

The descriptions that follow are based solely on your Sun and your Ascendant sign. Where matters such as inheritance or positions of authority are outlined for one Ascendant sign, it does not preclude another from such realizations when the whole chart is taken into consideration.

Remember, astrology is only your guide. You have the free will to choose what path you will take.

Chapter I

The Aries Ascendant Person

You have a proud erect posture and probably stand board straight. You have a lean firm physique and should remain in good form throughout your life. Possibly during your childhood you carried a little extra weight and in your senior years you will gain a little weight but people with an Aries Ascendant usually do not experience serious weight problems.

You walk fast and seem to slant forward as though to get as much speed as you can. You are an action person and programmed "fast." You think fast. You talk fast. You drive fast and haven't got much patience for those who don't. As a matter of fact, you have little or no patience. You even lose your temper fast and get over it fast but you don't hold a grudge. The other guy may be in shock but you are over it.

You have a quick wit and can be very humorous. You are a fast learner and can easily become bored and restless.

You could have blue eyes or light colored eyes. There is much expression in your eyes. They can be shining with love or laughter one moment but as soon as you become annoyed, they will start flashing fire. Your pride forbids you to give your feelings away but if one watches those bright eyes of yours, they will know what mood you are in.

You are probably fair and if your ancestry is from a dark-skinned race, you could have a lighter skin tone than others in your family.

Your head is broader at the temples and narrows down to your chin. Your hair may be thick and plentiful but men with this Ascendant sign frequently develop a bald spot as they grow older. Those possessing this Ascendant sign may have a somewhat conspicuous Adam's apple.

You have a keen sense of smell and can accurately detect various odors.

You are a proud person and tend to keep your true feelings hidden. You may even appear somewhat detached from a situation which is causing you stress. You could bring up to your stomach when emotionally upset and will probably suffer from ulcers at some time in your life.

You are prone to headaches and could experience rather severe headaches. You could have a scar or mark on your face or head area. You are able to tolerate high fevers better than most people and as a child undoubtedly endured some very high fevers.

When stressed, you sleep and the more stress you feel, the more you sleep. Listening to music relaxes you. In times of stress, you find comfort in a natural environment where there are trees and plants and the song of birds.

You will work for a well established corporation. You know the value of money and want security for yourself and your family. You work well under pressure.

You can be very sympathetic toward anyone with a tale of woe and will offer the shirt off your back to help. Be careful you are not taken advantage of.

You are fiercely independent but don't like to live alone. You will have a hobby or avocation which will bring much pleasure. At some time in your life, you could be involved in the world of entertainment, fashion or gambling.

You will travel extensively. You seem to be always on the go and usually in a hurry.

Aries Ascendant/Aries Sun

Your Sun is in the sign of Aries and if you were born within the time frame listed below, your Ascendant sign is also Aries.

Date of Birth	Time of Birth
March 21 to March 24	6:10 a.m. to 7:20 a.m.
March 25 to March 29	6:00 a.m. to 7:10 a.m.
March 30 to April 3	5:50 a.m. to 7:00 a.m.
April 4 to April 9	5:00 a.m. to 6:50 a.m.
April 10 to April 14	4:50 a.m. to 6:00 a.m.
April 15 to April 19	4:20 a.m. to 5:50 a.m.

You are the archetype for all Aries Ascendants. Your outline is the Aries Ascendant mold and everyone with the sign of Aries on the Ascendant is cast from this mold. The placement of the planets in a chart has a significant effect upon an individual but if the mold is cast in the form of an Aries, then that is how the child will grow.

Aries Ascendant/Taurus Sun

Your Sun is in the sign of Taurus and if you were born within the time frame listed below, your Ascendant sign is Aries.

Date of Birth	Time of Birth
April 20 to April 24	4:00 a.m. to 5:30 am
April 25 to April 28	3:50 a.m. to 5:10 am
April 29 to May 3	3:30 a.m. to 4:50 am
May 4 to May 9	3:15 a.m. to 4:20 am
May 10 to May 15	2:50 a.m. to 4:10 am
May 16 to May 20	2:30 a.m. to 3:50 am

Your Aries Ascendant makes you the fastest and most impatient Taurus of the whole zodiac. You have a pleasant voice and a natural sweetness in your smile. You recognize quality and want to have the best. There will come a time in your life when you will be involved in the world of entertainment, fashion or gambling.

Aries Ascendant/Gemini Sun

Your Sun is in the sign of Gemini and if you were born within the time frame listed below, your Ascendant sign is Aries.

Date of Birth	Time of Birth
May 21 to May 26	2:10 a.m. to 3:40 a.m.
May 27 to May 31	1:50 a.m. to 3:00 a.m.
June 1 to June 5	1:30 a.m. to 2:40 a.m.
June 6 to June 10	1:00 a.m. to 2:15 a.m.
June 11 to June 16	12:45 a.m. to 2:00 a.m.
June 17 to June 21	12:20 a.m. to 1:45 a.m.

You experience life in a state of perpetual activity. Aries and Gemini are two of the most active signs in the zodiac and with a Gemini Sun and an Aries Ascendant, you are a non-stop bundle of energy. You simply don't know how to remain idle for any appreciable length of time.

Aries Ascendant/Cancer Sun

Your Sun is in the sign of Cancer and if you were born within the time frame listed below, your Ascendant sign is Aries.

Date of Birth	Time of Birth
June 22 to June 27	12:10 a.m. to 1:40 a.m.
June 28 to Jun 30	11:30 p.m. to 1:10 a.m.
July 1 to July 5	11:15 p.m. to 12:50 a.m.
July 6 to July 10	11:00 p.m. to 12:15 a.m.
July 11 to July 16	10:30 p.m. to Midnight
July 17 to July 22	10:10 p.m. to 11:30 p.m.

You want a home you can be proud of. You will do most of your entertaining in your home and you could be an excellent cook. Your success in life will be more fully realized in your mature years.

Aries Ascendant/Leo Sun

Your Sun is in the sign of Leo and if you were born within the time frame listed below, your Ascendant sign is Aries.

Date of Birth	Time of Birth
July 23 to July 27	9:50 p.m. to 11:10 p.m.
July 28 to July 31	9:30 p.m. to 11:00 p.m.
August 1 to August 5	9:20 p.m. to 10:50 p.m.
August 6 to August 10	9:00 p.m. to 10:15 p.m.
August 11 to August 16	8:45 p.m. to 10:00 p.m.
August 17 to August 23	8:30 p.m. to 9:30 p.m.

You have a smile that lights up your whole face. You can be very determined once your mind is set. At some time in your life, you will be involved in the world of entertainment, fashion or gambling.

Aries Ascendant/Virgo Sun

Your Sun is in the sign of Virgo and if you were born within the time frame listed below, your Ascendant sign is Aries.

Date of Birth	Time of Birth
August 24 to August 28	7:50 p.m. to 9:20 p.m.
August 29 to August 31	7:30 p.m. to 8:50 p.m.
September 1 to September 5	7:20 p.m. to 8:20 p.m.
September 6 to September 10	7:00 p.m. to 8:10 p.m.
September 11 to September 17	6:40 p.m. to 7:50 p.m.
September 18 to September 22	6:20 p.m. to 7:20 p.m.

You take pride in your work and can be very analytical and detail minded in connection with your work. At some time in your life, you will attain a position of authority.

Aries Ascendant/Libra Sun

Your Sun is in the sign of Libra and if you were born within the time frame listed below, your Ascendant sign is Aries.

Date of Birth	Time of Birth
September 23 to September 27	5:50 p.m. to 7:10 p.m.
September 28 to September 30	5:40 p.m. to 7:00 p.m.
October 1 to October 5	5:20 p.m. to 6:50 p.m.
October 6 to October 10	5:00 p.m. to 6:15 p.m.
October 11 to October 17	4:30 p.m. to 6:00 p.m.
October 18 to October 23	4:15 p.m. to 5:50 p.m.

You will work with the public. You have a charming manner and a knack for handling people. You are a pleasant individual but you don't like anyone messing with your hair. You are particular about your hair and will either part it in the middle or have no definite part at all.

Aries Ascendant/Scorpio Sun

Your Sun is in the sign of Scorpio and if you were born within the time frame listed below, your Ascendant sign is Aries.

Date of Birth	Time of Birth
October 24 to October 28	3:50 p.m. to 5:10 p.m.
October 29 to October 31	3:40 p.m. to 5:00 p.m.
November 1 to November 6	3:20 p.m. to 4:50 p.m.
November 7 to November 12	3:00 p.m. to 4:20 p.m.
November 13 to November 18	2:30 p.m. to 4:00 p.m.
November 19 to November 22	2:10 p.m. to 3:40 p.m.

You have a strong interest in the mysteries of life and in the subject of life and the hereafter. You could receive money from the government and/or insurance benefits. There is a possibility you will receive an inheritance.

Aries Ascendant/Sagittarius Sun

Your Sun is in the sign of Sagittarius and if you were born within the time frame listed below, your Ascendant sign is Aries.

Date of Birth	Time of Birth
November 23 to November 27	1:50 p.m. to 3:10 p.m.
November 28 to December 1	1:30 p.m. to 3:00 p.m.
December 2 to December 6	1:15 p.m. to 2:50 p.m.
December 7 to December 11	1:00 p.m. to 2:20 p.m.
December 12 to December 16	12:40 p.m. to 2:00 p.m.
December 17 to December 21	12:20 p.m. to 1:40 p.m.

You are an enthusiastic, philosophical individual who has no patience for confining situations. You will travel the world and could live in a distant or foreign land at some time in your life.

Aries Ascendant/Capricorn Sun

Your Sun is in the sign of Capricorn and if you were born within the time frame listed below, your Ascendant sign is Aries.

Date of Birth	Time of Birth
December 22 to December 26	12:00 Noon to 1:30 p.m.
December 27 to December 31	11:50 a.m. to 1:10 p.m.
January 1 to January 4	11:20 a.m. to 12:50 p.m.
January 5 to January 10	11:00 a.m. to 12:20 p.m.
January 11 to January 15	10:45 a.m. to 12:00 Noon
January 16 to January 19	10:15 a.m. to 11:50 am

You take pride in your work and at some time in your life will attain a position of authority. Those born with the Sun in Capricorn often appear old when they are young and young when they are old. You may have endured some restriction or responsibility in your youth which prevented a carefree childhood.

Aries Ascendant/Aquarius Sun

Your Sun is in the sign of Aquarius and if you were born within the time frame listed below, your Ascendant sign is Aries.

Date of Birth	Time of Birth
January 20 to January 24	10:00 a.m. to 11:50 a.m.
January 25 to January 29	9:50 a.m. to 11:10 a.m.
January 30 to February 2	9:20 a.m. to 11:00 a.m.
February 3 to February 7	9:10 a.m. to 10:50 a.m.
February 8 to February 12	9:00 a.m. to 10:10 a.m.
February 13 to February 18	8:50 a.m. to 10:00 a.m.

Friendships are important to you. You will have a friend who is quite independent and a friend whose thinking is rather advanced. You will have a particular friend who will be very meaningful to you. You will enjoy a position of leadership among your friends.

Aries Ascendant/Pisces Sun

Your Sun is in the sign of Pisces and if you were born within the time frame listed below, your Ascendant sign is Aries.

Date of Birth	Time of Birth
February 19 to February 23	8:20 a.m. to 9:20 am
February 24 to February 27	7:50 a.m. to 9:10 am
February 28 to March 3	7:20 a.m. to 9:00 am
March 4 to March 9	7:10 a.m. to 8:50 am
March 10 to March 14	7:00 a.m. to 8:10 am
March 15 to March 20	6:20 a.m. to 8:00 am

You have much interest in the mysteries of life. You were shy in your youth. There was some situation which caused unhappiness in your formative years. There may have been an illness or a separation from someone dear to you which made you feel lonely or unloved at a tender age.

Chapter II

The Taurus Ascendant Person

You have a pleasant voice and a sweet smile and could have dimples. There is a natural sweetness to your nature which belies the incredible determination of your will. Some may even say you are bull-headed. You have much patience and the perseverance to wait for what you want in life. At times this can mean digging in your heels and stubbornly refusing to budge on an issue until you get what you want.

You have a deep-chested physique and your flesh is hard and firm. Your shoulders are broad and you have a short thick neck. Your hair has a natural curl or you wear your hair in a style which covers part of your forehead.

Your eyes tend to have an almost child-like expression and you notice people; you follow them around with your eyes. Those with the sign of Taurus on the Ascendant will often have large beautiful eyes. There is however a Taurus Ascendant type with noticeably small eyes.

Taurus on the Ascendant will seldom give large ears. You could have heavy ear lobes but it is more probable that your ears will be small. Your nose is compact and the nostrils could be wide or have a slight flair. You have full sensual lips.

You have a steady, easy going temperament and rarely show annoyance. You are perfectly content to relax and luxuriate in the privacy of your own home.

There is, however, a Taurus Ascendant type with a highly nervous and excitable nature. This type can be just as pleasant as the easy going Taurus but they constantly seek perfection in some area of their lives and they easily become anxious and agitated when things are not to their liking.

There seems to be a physical difference between the excitable Taurus Ascendant and the patient Taurus Ascendant. This highly nervous type may not be as broad in the shoulders as the patient Taurus Ascendant. Their lips may not be as full, or possibly their neck could be slim rather than the short thick neck found on the more patient type. In this case, the patience for which Taurus is so well known may be found more on the part of those connected with this high-strung type.

The excitable Taurus Ascendant person could use his or her nervous energy in working on some project at home. If this type does not have a pet project to work on at home, he or she may not enjoy staying home at all.

Whether you are the calm patient Taurus Ascendant or the highly excitable Taurus Ascendant, you have an excellent memory, especially of your childhood years. You are security minded and very sensitive. You have the type of mind which thinks fast in emergency situations. Your thoughts will often be focused on ways to make money for yourself and your family. You will have more than one way of earning an income during your lifetime.

You want your work to be a little different than the usual. You want your work to be interesting and could have some type of recreational benefit or other type of benefit in connection with your work. You could work in a partnership. You will make a rather sudden change in your career at some point in your life.

You are able to communicate very well with the public and are sensitive to the needs of the public. You will travel and there may be travel involved with your work.

You want a good home for your family and a house you can be proud of. You enjoy the creature comforts and want a home with pleasant surroundings. You prefer to live in an area with lots of trees and plants. You like to entertain in your home. You enjoy good food and could be an excellent cook.

Taurus Ascendant/Aries Sun

Your Sun is in the sign of Aries and if you were born within the time frame listed below, your Ascendant sign is Taurus.

Date of Birth	Time of Birth
March 21 to March 24	7:20 a.m. to 9:00 a.m.
March 25 to March 29	7:10 a.m. to 8:50 a.m.
March 30 to April 3	7:00 a.m. to 8:20 a.m.
April 4 to April 9	6:50 a.m. to 8:10 a.m.
April 10 to April 14	6:10 a.m. to 7:20 a.m.
April 15 to April 19	6:00 a.m. to 7:10 a.m.

Your fast paced Aries Sun develops patience as it finds expression through your slower moving Taurus Ascendant. You were shy in your youth. There was some situation which caused unhappiness in your formative years. There may have been an illness or a separation from someone dear to you which made you feel lonely or unloved at a tender age.

Taurus Ascendant/Taurus Sun

Your Sun is in the sign of Taurus and if you were born within the time frame listed below, your Ascendant sign is also Taurus.

Date of Birth	Time of Birth
April 20 to April 24	5:20 a.m. to 7:00 a.m.
April 25 to April 28	5:10 a.m. to 6:30 a.m.
April 29 to May 3	4:50 a.m. to 6:15 a.m.
May 4 to May 9	4:20 a.m. to 6:00 a.m.
May 10 to May 15	4:10 a.m. to 5:45 a.m.
May 16 to May 20	3:50 a.m. to 5:10 a.m.

You are the archetype for all Taurus Ascendants. Your outline is the Taurus Ascendant mold and everyone with the sign of Taurus on the Ascendant is cast from this mold. The placement of the planets in a chart has a significant effect upon an individual but if the mold is cast in the form of a Taurus, then that is how the child will grow.

Taurus Ascendant/Gemini Sun

Your Sun is in the sign of Gemini and if you were born within the time frame listed below, your Ascendant sign is Taurus.

Date of Birth	Time of Birth
May 21 to May 26	3:40 a.m. to 5:00 a.m.
May 27 to May 31	3:00 a.m. to 4:30 a.m.
June 1 to June 5	2:40 a.m. to 4:10 a.m.
June 6 to June 10	2:15 a.m. to 3:50 a.m.
June 11 to June 16	2:00 a.m. to 3:40 a.m.
June 17 to June 21	1:45 a.m. to 3:10 a.m.

You will have more than one way of making money. Your thinking is directed toward security. You recognize quality and want to have the best. At some time in your life, you will be involved in the world of entertainment, fashion or gambling.

Taurus Ascendant/Cancer Sun

Your Sun is in the sign of Cancer and if you were born within the time frame listed below, your Ascendant sign is Taurus.

Date of Birth	Time of Birth
June 22 to Jun 27	1:40 a.m. to 2:50 a.m.
June 28 to Jun 30	1:10 a.m. to 2:30 a.m.
July 1 to July 5	12:50 a.m. to 2:15 a.m.
July 6 to July 10	12:15 a.m. to 2:00 a.m.
July 11 to July 16	Midnight to 1:20 a.m.
July 17 to July 22	11:30 p.m. to 1:00 a.m.

You have a sensitive understanding of people and could be a gifted storyteller. Your thoughts are frequently on your home and your family. You may travel but you will always be glad to return home.

Taurus Ascendant/Leo Sun

Your Sun is in the sign of Leo and if you were born within the
time frame listed below, your Ascendant sign is Taurus.

Date of Birth	Time of Birth
July 23 to July 27	11:10 p.m. to 12:50 a.m.
July 28 to July 31	11:00 p.m. to 12:30 a.m.
August 1 to August 5	10:50 p.m. to 12:10 a.m.
August 6 to August 10	10:15 p.m. to Midnight
August 11 to August 16	10:00 p.m. to 11:20 a.m.
August 17 to August 23	9:30 p.m. to 11:00 a.m.

The combination of a Leo Sun and a Taurus Ascendant gives
much determination. You want a home you can be proud of and
you will prefer to entertain in your home. You will be the head
of your household. Your success in life will be more fully realized
in your mature years.

Taurus Ascendant/Virgo Sun

Your Sun is in the sign of Virgo and if you were born within the
time frame listed below, your Ascendant sign is Taurus.

Date of Birth	Time of Birth
August 24 to August 28	9:20 p.m. to 10:40 p.m.
August 29 to August 31	8:50 p.m. to 10:10 p.m.
September 1 to September 5	8:20 p.m. to 10:00 p.m.
September 6 to September 10	8:10 p.m. to 9:50 p.m.
September 11 to September 17	7:50 p.m. to 9:15 p.m.
September 18 to September 22	7:20 p.m. to 9:00 p.m.

You could be very creative. You are very analytical and detail
minded. At some time in your life, you will be involved in the
world of entertainment, fashion or gambling.

Taurus Ascendant/Libra Sun

Your Sun is in the sign of Libra and if you were born within the time frame listed below, your Ascendant sign is Taurus.

Date of Birth	Time of Birth
September 23 to September 27	7:10 p.m. to 8:50 p.m.
September 28 to September 30	7:00 p.m. to 8:20 p.m.
October 1 to October 5	6:50 p.m. to 8:10 p.m.
October 6 to October 10	6:15 p.m. to 7:30 p.m.
October 11 to October 17	6:00 p.m. to 7:15 p.m.
October 18 to October 23	5:50 p.m. to 7:05 p.m.

You take pride in your work and can be analytical and detail minded in connection with your work. You could attain a position of authority. You dislike boring physical labor. You have a charming personality but you are particular about your hair and don't like anyone messing with it.

Taurus Ascendant/Scorpio Sun

Your Sun is in the sign of Scorpio and if you were born within the time frame listed below, your Ascendant sign is Taurus.

Date of Birth	Time of Birth
October 24 to October 28	5:10 p.m. to 7:00 p.m.
October 29 to October 31	5:00 p.m. to 6:30 p.m.
November 1 to November 6	4:50 p.m. to 6:20 p.m.
November 7 to November 12	4:20 p.m. to 6:00 p.m.
November 13 to November 18	4:00 p.m. to 5:50 p.m.
November 19 to November 22	3:40 p.m. to 5:10 p.m.

You will work with the public. You have a knack for handling people and an intuitive sensitivity to the needs of the public. At some time in your life you will work in a partnership.

Taurus Ascendant/Sagittarius Sun

Your Sun is in the sign of Sagittarius and if you were born within the time frame listed below, your Ascendant sign is Taurus.

Date of Birth	Time of Birth
November 23 to November 27	3:10 p.m. to 4:30 p.m.
November 28 to December 1	3:00 p.m. to 4:20 p.m.
December 2 to December 6	2:50 p.m. to 4:10 p.m.
December 7 to December 11	2:20 p.m. to 4:00 p.m.
December 12 to December 16	2:00 p.m. to 3:20 p.m.
December 17 to December 21	1:40 p.m. to 3:10 p.m.

You have a strong interest in the mysteries of life and in the subject of life and the hereafter. You could receive money from the government and/or insurance benefits. There is a possibility you will receive an inheritance.

Taurus Ascendant/Capricorn Sun

Your Sun is in the sign of Capricorn and if you were born within the time frame listed below, your Ascendant sign is Taurus.

Date of Birth	Time of Birth
December 22 to December 26	1:30 p.m. to 3:00 p.m.
December 27 to December 31	1:10 p.m. to 2:45 p.m.
January 1 to January 4	12:50 p.m. to 2:10 p.m.
January 5 to January 10	12:20 p.m. to 2:00 p.m.
January 11 to January 15	12:00 Noon to 1:50 p.m.
January 16 to January 19	11:50 a.m. to 1:10 p.m.

Those born with the Sun in Capricorn often appear old when they are young and young when they are old. You may have endured some restriction or responsibility in your youth which prevented a carefree childhood. There is a possibility you will make your home in a distant or foreign land at some point in your life.

Taurus Ascendant/Aquarius Sun

Your Sun is in the sign of Aquarius and if you were born within the time frame listed below, your Ascendant sign is Taurus.

Date of Birth	Time of Birth
January 20 to January 24	11:50 a.m. to 1:00 p.m.
January 25 to January 29	11:10 a.m. to 12:20 p.m.
January 30 to February 2	11:00 a.m. to 12:10 p.m.
February 3 to February 7	10:50 a.m. to 12:00 Noon
February 8 to February 12	10:10 a.m. to 11:50 a.m.
February 13 to February 18	10:00 a.m. to 11:15 a.m.

You take pride in your work and want a position you can be proud of. Your career and your home seem to be intermingled. At some time in your life, you will attain a position of authority.

Taurus Ascendant/Pisces Sun

Your Sun is in the sign of Pisces and if you were born within the time frame listed below, your Ascendant sign is Taurus.

Date of Birth	Time of Birth
February 19 to February 23	9:20 a.m. to 11:00 a.m.
February 24 to February 27	9:10 a.m. to 10:30 a.m.
February 28 to Mar 3	9:00 a.m. to 10:20 a.m.
March 4 to March 9	8:50 a.m. to 10:10 a.m.
March 10 to March 14	8:10 a.m. to 10:00 a.m.
March 15 to March 20	8:00 a.m. to 9:20 a.m.

Friendships are important to you. Your friends tend to be of a sensitive nature. You will have a particular friend you will care for very much. At some time in your life you will feel much sorrow over a friend.

Chapter III

The Gemini Ascendant Person

You have a slender physique and long slim legs. You also have long slim fingers and a habit of gesturing with your hands when in conversation. You have a keen sense of touch and like the feel of fine fabrics and good materials.

You are light on your feet and have a fast-paced step with a tendency to break into a run as you walk.

You could part your hair in the middle or on the side or have no definite part at all and will probably try all three styles at various times in your life.

The expression in your eyes gives the sensation of being on the alert like a bird or a deer whose eyes seem to sense the environment. Your mouth is not overly large and could be considered small or regular in size. Your top lip may be slightly more prominent than your lower lip. Gemini Ascendant individuals do not have large chins and never have double chins.

With the sign of Gemini on your Ascendant, you are a pleasant individual with much nervous energy. You will always be busy working on some project and seem to relax by working on your projects. You are impatient and will have a number of things going on at the same time. You become enthused over different activities and try to fit them all on your agenda but when there isn't time to do everything, you drop the ones that least interest you. The symbol for Gemini is the twins and you keep yourself busy enough for two people.

The Gemini symbol of the twins aptly describes the fact that there are two types classified under this Ascendant sign. There is the talkative type and the quiet type. They are both inquisitive and it is indeed possible for the talkative type to turn into the quiet

17

type at some stage. You could be talkative at work and quiet at home or it may be that you are talkative in your youth and quiet in your maturity. In one area of your life or one stage of your life, you will be talkative and in another quiet.

You can be clannish in connection with family members and probably have memories of someone in your family, possibly your mother, who was particular about keeping a clean and tidy house.

You will always have at least one particularly good friend. You will have a very independent friend and a friend who will have a mark or scar on the face or head area. You will have a friend who suffers from migraine headaches. You will travel with a friend. When you go out, you like to go first class.

You are quite intuitive concerning the public and can anticipate the needs of the public. You will work with the public and could work for the government. At some point in your career, you will work from your home. You could have a natural talent for teaching or writing.

You will experience a number of changes in your workplace or in the projects you work on. You are emotionally adaptable to change.

You will receive money from the government and there is a possibility you will receive an inheritance. There will come a time when you will become very emotional in connection with a money matter.

At some time in your life, you will receive sudden or unexpected news from afar and may have to make travel arrangements on short notice.

With the youthful, inquisitive sign of Gemini on your Ascendant, you will keep actively busy throughout your lifetime.

Gemini Ascendant/Aries Sun

Your Sun is in the sign of Aries and if you were born within the time frame listed below, your Ascendant sign is Gemini.

Date of Birth	Time of Birth
March 21 to March 24	9:00 a.m. to 11:00 a.m.
March 25 to March 29	8:50 a.m. to 10:20 a.m.
March 30 to April 3	8:20 a.m. to 10:10 a.m.
April 4 to April 9	8:10 a.m. to 10:00 a.m.
April 10 to April 14	7:20 a.m. to 9:20 a.m.
April 15 to April 19	7:10 a.m. to 9:10 a.m.

You are a whirlwind of activity. There are not too many who are able to keep up with you. You like action people. Your friendships are important to you and there will be a particularly meaningful friendship in your life.

Gemini Ascendant/Taurus Sun

Your Sun is in the sign of Taurus and if you were born within the time frame listed below, your Ascendant sign is Gemini.

Date of Birth	Time of Birth
April 20 to April 24	7:00 a.m. to 8:45 a.m.
April 25 to April 28	6:30 a.m. to 8:30 a.m.
April 29 to May 3	6:15 a.m. to 8:15 a.m.
May 4 to May 9	6:00 a.m. to 8:00 a.m.
May 10 to May 15	5:45 a.m. to 7:30 a.m.
May 16 to May 20	5:10 a.m. to 7:00 a.m.

You have a strong interest in the mysteries of life. You were shy in your youth. Some situation in your young years caused unhappiness. There could have been a health problem or a separation from a loved one which made you feel lonely or unloved at a tender age.

Gemini Ascendant/Gemini Sun

Your Sun is in the sign of Gemini and if you were born within the time frame listed below, your Ascendant sign is also Gemini.

Date of Birth	Time of Birth
May 21 to May 26	5:00 a.m. to 7:00 a.m.
May 27 to May 31	4:30 a.m. to 6:20 a.m.
June 1 to June 5	4:10 a.m. to 6:10 a.m.
June 6 to June 10	3:50 a.m. to 5:50 a.m.
June 11 to June 16	3:40 a.m. to 5:20 a.m.
June 17 to June 21	3:10 a.m. to 5:10 a.m.

You are the archetype for all Gemini Ascendants. Your outline is the Gemini Ascendant mold and everyone with the sign of Gemini on the Ascendant is cast from this mold. The placement of the planets in a chart has a significant effect upon an individual but if the mold is cast in the form of a Gemini, then that is how the child will grow.

Gemini Ascendant/Cancer Sun

Your Sun is in the sign of Cancer and if you were born within the time frame listed below, your Ascendant sign is Gemini.

Date of Birth	Time of Birth
June 22 to June 27	2:50 a.m. to 5:00 a.m.
June 28 to June 30	2:30 a.m. to 4:20 a.m.
July 1 to July 5	2:15 a.m. to 4:10 a.m.
July 6 to July 10	2:00 a.m. to 3:50 a.m.
July 11 to July 16	1:20 a.m. to 3:10 a.m.
July 17 to Jul 22	1:00 a.m. to 3:00 a.m.

You are sensitive and could have an intuitive grasp on the thinking of the general public. At some time in your life, you will be involved in the world of entertainment, fashion or gambling. You recognize quality and want the best.

Gemini Ascendant/Leo Sun

Your Sun is in the sign of Leo and if you were born within the time frame listed below, your Ascendant sign is Gemini.

Date of Birth	Time of Birth
July 23 to July 27	12:50 a.m. to 2:30 a.m.
July 28 to July 31	12:30 a.m. to 2:10 a.m.
August 1 to August 5	12:10 a.m. to 2:00 a.m.
August 6 to August 10	Midnight to 1:50 a.m.
August 11 to August 16	11:20 p.m. to 1:15 a.m.
August 17 to August 23	11:00 p.m. to 1:00 a.m.

You have a rather dramatic presence and a smile that lights up your whole face. You will have a desire to communicate in some way and you will travel. You can be extremely determined once your mind is set.

Gemini Ascendant/Virgo Sun

Your Sun is in the sign of Virgo and if you were born within the time frame listed below, your Ascendant sign is Gemini.

Date of Birth	Time of Birth
August 24 to August 28	10:40 p.m. to 12:40 a.m.
August 29 to August 31	10:10 p.m. to 12:10 a.m.
September 1 to September 5	10:00 p.m. to 12:05 a.m.
September 6 to September 10	9:50 p.m. to Midnight
September 11 to September 17	9:15 p.m. to 11:50 p.m.
September 18 to September 22	9:00 p.m. to 11:15 p.m.

You want a home you can be proud of and will do most of your entertaining in your home. At some time in your life, you will work from your home. You have an analytical nature and your success in life will be more fully realized in your mature years.

Gemini Ascendant/Libra Sun

Your Sun is in the sign of Libra and if you were born within the time frame listed below, your Ascendant sign is Gemini.

Date of Birth	Time of Birth
September 23 to September 27	8:50 p.m. to 10:40 p.m.
September 28 to September 30	8:20 p.m. to 10:20 p.m.
October 1 to October 5	8:10 p.m. to 10:05 p.m.
October 6 to October 10	7:30 p.m. to 9:30 p.m.
October 11 to October 17	7:15 p.m. to 9:15 p.m.
October 18 to October 23	7:05 p.m. to 9:00 p.m.

You are creative and have a distinct dislike for boring physical labor. At some time in your life, you will be involved in the world of entertainment, fashion or gambling. You are particular about your hair and don't like anyone messing with it.

Gemini Ascendant/Scorpio Sun

Your Sun is in the sign of Scorpio and if you were born within the time frame listed below, your Ascendant sign is Gemini.

Date of Birth	Time of Birth
October 24 to October 28	7:00 p.m. to 8:50 p.m.
October 29 to October 31	6:30 p.m. to 8:20 p.m.
November 1 to November 6	6:20 p.m. to 8:10 p.m.
November 7 to November 12	6:00 p.m. to 8:00 p.m.
November 13 to November 18	5:50 p.m. to 7:20 p.m.
November 19 to November 22	5:10 p.m. to 7:10 p.m.

You take pride in your work. You are analytical and detail minded in connection with your work. At some time in your life, you will attain a position of authority.

Gemini Ascendant/Sagittarius Sun

Your Sun is in the sign of Sagittarius and if you were born within the time frame listed below, your Ascendant sign is Gemini.

Date of Birth	Time of Birth
November 23 to November 27	4:30 p.m. to 6:50 p.m.
November 28 to December 1	4:20 p.m. to 6:20 p.m.
December 2 to December 6	4:10 p.m. to 6:10 p.m.
December 7 to December 11	4:00 p.m. to 6:00 p.m.
December 12 to December 16	3:20 p.m. to 5:20 p.m.
December 17 to December 21	3:10 p.m. to 5:10 p.m.

You have enthusiasm and a natural charm. You have a way with people and will find success working with the public. You are quite witty and enjoy working with people. You will work in a partnership at some time in your life.

Gemini Ascendant/Capricorn Sun

Your Sun is in the sign of Capricorn and if you were born within the time frame listed below, your Ascendant sign is Gemini.

Date of Birth	Time of Birth
December 22 to December 26	3:00 p.m. to 4:50 p.m.
December 27 to December 31	2:45 p.m. to 4:20 p.m.
January 1 to January 4	2:10 p.m. to 4:10 p.m.
January 5 to January 10	2:00 p.m. to 4:00 p.m.
January 11 to January 15	1:50 p.m. to 3:50 p.m.
January 16 to January 19	1:10 p.m. to 3:10 p.m.

Those born with the Sun in Capricorn often appear old when they are young and young when they are old. You may have endured some restriction or responsibility in your youth which prevented a carefree childhood. You could receive money from the government and it is possible that you will receive an inheritance. You have a strong interest in the mysteries of life.

Gemini Ascendant/Aquarius Sun

Your Sun is in the sign of Aquarius and if you were born within the time frame listed below, your Ascendant sign is Gemini.

Date of Birth	Time of Birth
January 20 to January 24	1:00 p.m. to 3:00 p.m.
January 25 to January 29	12:20 p.m. to 2:50 p.m.
January 30 to February 2	12:10 p.m. to 2:10 p.m.
January 3 to February 7	12:00 Noon to 2:00 p.m.
February 8 to February 12	11:50 a.m. to 1:50 p.m.
February 13 to February 18	11:15 a.m. to 1:20 p.m.

You will travel to faraway places. You could make your home in a distant or foreign land. As you mature, you will develop a philosophical outlook on life. You could have a natural talent for teaching or writing.

Gemini Ascendant/Pisces Sun

Your Sun is in the sign of Pisces and if you were born within the time frame listed below, your Ascendant sign is Gemini.

Date of Birth	Time of Birth
February 19 to February 23	11:00 a.m. to 1:00 p.m.
February 24 to February 27	10:30 a.m. to 12:20 p.m.
February 28 to March 3	10:20 a.m. to 12:10 p.m.
Mar 4 to March 9	10:10 a.m. to 12:00 Noon
Mar 10 to March 14	10:00 a.m. to 11:50 a.m.
Mar 15 to March 20	9:20 a.m. to 11:10 a.m.

You take pride in your work. Most of your energies will be directed into your work. At some time in your life, you will attain a position of authority.

Chapter IV

The Cancer Ascendant Person

Y ou have a warm compassionate nature and can be very sympathetic and understanding. You are intuitive.

You feel emotions strongly and are quite sensitive to criticism. You feel mood swings. This is because the moon rules the sign of Cancer and the moon is changeable. On its path through the heavens, the moon will travel through each sign of the zodiac, staying in a sign for about two and a half days. Sometimes you can actually feel the difference as the moon travels from one sign to the next. Your mood will change as the moon changes signs.

You have a nicely rounded physique with no sharp corners. With the sign of Cancer on your Ascendant, you will gain weight easily. Unless a diet is carefully adhered to, you could become pleasingly plump or just plain fat. Men with a Cancer Ascendant usually develop love handles. You enjoy good food and could be a good cook.

Your hands are soft and small and your fingers are short. Cancer Ascendant people have small or short feet. Your walk is a type of leisurely stroll.

You have a quiet voice and well-shaped lips. You have a soft full face and your complexion is fair or pale. This Ascendant sign gives a plentiful head of hair.

Very often individuals with the sign of Cancer on their Ascendant will have beautiful dreamy looking eyes. You can be somewhat of a day-dreamer and you really love to sleep.

You have a good memory, especially of your younger years and may have a tendency to dwell on the past. An older woman, possibly your grandmother, played a prominent role in your formative years. You have a parent who is considered very attractive.

You are analytical and detail minded and dislike confusion in either your thinking or your surroundings.

You can be a calming influence and are basically a home-loving person. You need peace and harmony in your home in order to maintain your equilibrium. Ideally, you want a home with plenty of space to move around in.

You are rather independent in your work and capable of working on your own. You definitely do not like someone supervising you or telling you what to do.

You have a pleasant agreeable manner but will rebel in no uncertain terms if you feel someone is attempting to boss you.

You have a tendency to wait until the last minute to prepare what is needed for your work or it could be that you do not receive the information needed for your work until the last minute. Somehow there is a time pressure involved in what you do. You will find that you perform at your best when under pressure. You are adept at making snap decisions when necessary.

You will work with people from all walks of life. You have a good personality for dealing with the public. You have a caring nature and the ability to sympathize with others. There could be travel involved with your work. You will keep records or books. You take pride in your work and at some point in your career, you will attain a position of authority.

You will have a friend who is extremely stubborn and a friend who is very wealthy. You will mingle with wealthy and influential people.

You recognize quality and like to have the best. During your lifetime, you will be involved in some way with the world of entertainment, fashion or gambling.

Cancer Ascendant/Aries Sun

Your Sun is in the sign of Aries and if you were born within the time frame listed below, your Ascendant sign is Cancer.

Date of Birth	Time of Birth
March 21 to March 24	11:00 a.m. to 1:10 p.m.
March 25 to March 29	10:20 a.m. to 1:00 p.m.
March 30 to April 3	10:10 a.m. to 12:50 p.m.
April 4 to April 9	10:00 a.m. to 12:10 p.m.
April 10 to April 14	9:20 a.m. to 12:00 Noon
April 15 to Apr 19	9:10 a.m. to 11:50 a.m.

You take pride in your work and want a career you can be proud of. You will direct most of your energies into your work. At some point in your life, you will attain a position of authority.

Cancer Ascendant/Taurus Sun

Your Sun is in the sign of Taurus and if you were born within the time frame listed below, your Ascendant sign is Cancer.

Date of Birth	Time of Birth
April 20 to April 24	8:45 a.m. to 11:15 a.m.
April 25 to April 28	8:30 a.m. to 11:00 a.m.
April 29 to May 3	8:15 a.m. to 10:30 a.m.
May 4 to May 9	8:00 a.m. to 10:15 a.m.
May 10 to May 15	7:30 a.m. to 10:00 a.m.
May 16 to May 20	7:00 a.m. to 9:45 a.m.

Friendships are important to you. Your friends tend to be determined individuals. You will have a friend who is extremely stubborn and a friend who is very wealthy. You will have financial dealings with a friend.

Cancer Ascendant/Gemini Sun

Your Sun is in the sign of Gemini and if you were born within the time frame listed below, your Ascendant sign is Cancer.

Date of Birth	Time of Birth
May 21 to May 26	7:00 a.m. to 9:10 a.m
May 27 to May 31	6:20 a.m. to 8:30 a.m
June 1 to June 5	6:10 a.m. to 8:15 a.m
June 6 to June 10	5:50 a.m. to 8:00 a.m
June 11 to June 16	5:20 a.m. to 7:50 a.m.
June 17 to June 21	5:10 a.m. to 7:10 a.m.

You were shy in your youth. There was some situation which caused unhappiness in your formative years. There could have been a health problem or a separation from someone dear to you which made you feel lonely or unloved at a tender age. You have a strong interest in the mysteries of life.

Cancer Ascendant/Cancer Sun

Your Sun is in the sign of Cancer and if you were born within the time frame listed below, your Ascendant sign is also Cancer.

Date of Birth	Time of Birth
June 22 to June 27	5:00 a.m. to 7:10 a.m.
June 28 to June 30	4:20 a.m. to 7:00 a.m.
July 1 to July 5	4:10 a.m. to 6:20 a.m.
July 6 to July 10	3:50 a.m. to 6:15 a.m.
July 11 to Jul 16	3:10 a.m. to 6:00 a.m.
July 17 to Jul 22	3:00 a.m. to 5:50 a.m.

You are the archetype for all Cancer Ascendants. Your outline is the Cancer Ascendant mold and everyone with the sign of Cancer on the Ascendant is cast from this mold. The placement of the planets in a chart has a significant effect upon an individual but if the mold is cast in the form of a Cancer, then that is how the child will grow.

Cancer Ascendant/Leo Sun

Your Sun is in the sign of Leo and if you were born within the time frame listed below, your Ascendant sign is Cancer.

Date of Birth	Time of Birth
July 23 to July 27	2:30 a.m. to 5:10 a.m.
July 28 to July 31	2:10 a.m. to 5:00 a.m.
August 1 to August 5	2:00 a.m. to 4:20 a.m.
August 6 to August 10	1:50 am to 4:10 a.m.
August 11 to August 16	1:15 a.m. to 4:00 a.m.
August 17 to August 23	1:00 a.m. to 3:15 a.m.

You have a smile that lights up your whole face. You recognize quality and want the best. You have determination and at some time in your life will be involved in the world of entertainment, fashion or gambling.

Cancer Ascendant/Virgo Sun

Your Sun is in the sign of Virgo and if you were born within the time frame listed below, your Ascendant sign is Cancer.

Date of Birth	Time of Birth
August 24 to August 28	12:40 a.m. to 2:50 a.m.
August 29 to August 31	12:10 a.m. to 2:30 a.m.
September 1 to September 5	12:05 a.m. to 2:20 a.m.
September 6 to September 10	Midnight to 2:10 a.m.
September 11 to September 17	11:50 p.m. to 2:00 a.m.
September 18 to September 22	11:15 p.m. to 1:50 a.m.

Your mind is always working. You will want to express yourself in some way. You could have a natural talent for teaching or writing. The subject of health or diet may be of special interest to you.

Cancer Ascendant/Libra Sun

Your Sun is in the sign of Libra and if you were born within the time frame listed below, your Ascendant sign is Cancer.

Date of Birth	Time of Birth
September 23 to September 27	10:40 p.m. to 1:10 a.m.
September 28 to September 30	10:20 p.m. to 1:00 a.m.
October 1 to October 5	10:05 p.m. to 12:50 a.m.
October 6 to October 10	9:30 p.m. to 12:15 a.m.
October 11 to October 17	9:15 p.m. to Midnight
October 18 to October 23	9:00 p.m. to 11:30 p.m.

You have a charming manner. You want a home with lots of space and you are probably an excellent cook. You could work from your home. You could also work in a partnership. Your success in life will be more fully realized in your mature years. You are particular about your hair and don't like anyone messing with it.

Cancer Ascendant/Scorpio Sun

Your Sun is in the sign of Scorpio and if you were born within the time frame listed below, your Ascendant sign is Cancer.

Date of Birth	Time of Birth
October 24 to October 28	8:50 p.m. to 11:00 p.m.
October 29 to October 31	8:20 p.m. to 10:50 p.m.
November 1 to November 6	8:10 p.m. to 10:20 p.m.
November 7 to November 12	8:00 p.m. to 10:10 p.m.
November 13 to November 18	7:20 p.m. to 9:50 p.m.
November 19 to November 22	7:10 p.m. to 9:20 p.m.

You can be very creative. You are intuitive and have strong emotions. You are also determined and at some time in your life will be involved in the world of entertainment, fashion or gambling.

Cancer Ascendant/Sagittarius Sun

Your Sun is in the sign of Sagittarius and if you were born within the time frame listed below, your Ascendant sign is Cancer.

Date of Birth	Time of Birth
November 23 to November 27	6:50 p.m. to 9:00 p.m.
November 28 to December 1	6:20 p.m. to 8:50 p.m.
December 2 to December 6	6:10 p.m. to 8:20 p.m.
December 7 to December 11	6:00 p.m. to 8:10 p.m.
December 12 to December 16	5:20 p.m. to 8:00 p.m.
December 17 to December 21	5:10 p.m. to 7:20 p.m.

You take pride in your work. You are analytical and detail minded in connection with your work. You could travel. You will be involved with people from all walks of life and at some time in your life, you will attain a position of authority.

Cancer Ascendant/Capricorn Sun

Your Sun is in the sign of Capricorn and if you were born within the time frame listed below, your Ascendant sign is Cancer.

Date of Birth	Time of Birth
December 22 to December 26	4:50 p.m. to 7:10 p.m.
December 27 to December 31	4:20 p.m. to 7:00 p.m.
January 1 to January 4	4:10 p.m. to 6:20 p.m.
January 5 to January 10	4:00 p.m. to 6:10 p.m.
January 11 to January 15	3:50 p.m. to 6:00 p.m.
January 16 to January 19	3:10 p.m. to 5:20 p.m.

Those born with the Sun in Capricorn often appear old when they are young and young when they are old. You may have endured some restriction or responsibility in your young years which prevented a carefree childhood. You have a charming manner and will find success in working with the public.

Cancer Ascendant/Aquarius Sun

Your Sun is in the sign of Aquarius and if you were born within the time frame listed below, your Ascendant sign is Cancer.

Date of Birth	Time of Birth
January 20 to January 24	3:00 p.m. to 5:10 p.m.
January 25 to January 29	2:50 p.m. to 5:00 p.m.
January 30 to February 2	2:10 p.m. to 4:50 p.m.
February 3 to February 7	2:00 p.m. to 4:10 p.m.
February 8 to February 12	1:50 p.m. to 4:00 p.m.
February 13 to February 18	1:20 p.m. to 3:50 p.m.

You have a strong interest in the mysteries of life and in the subject of life and the hereafter. There is a possibility you will receive an inheritance which could have an element of surprise connected to it.

Cancer Ascendant/Pisces Sun

Your Sun is in the sign of Pisces and if you were born within the time frame listed below, your Ascendant sign is Cancer.

Date of Birth	Time of Birth
February 19 to February 23	1:00 p.m. to 3:10 p.m.
February 24 to February 27	12:20 p.m. to 3:00 p.m.
February 28 to March 3	12:10 p.m. to 2:50 p.m.
March 4 to March 9	12:00 Noon to 2:20 p.m.
March 10 to March 14	11:50 a.m. to 2:10 p.m.
March 15 to March 20	11:10 a.m. to 2:00 p.m.

At some time in your life, you will live in a distant or foreign land. You could have a natural talent for teaching or writing. You will become quite philosophical in your mature years.

Chapter V

The Leo Ascendant Person

You have a firm deep-chested physique with a good shoulder line and a torso that slims down to the hips. It is said that the Leo physique is cone-shaped or carrot-shaped. However it seems more appropriate to compare the form of a Leo with that of the lion, Leo's astrological symbol. The lion's upper body is large with his magnificent mane and powerful chest. The body of a Leo Ascendant individual has broad shoulders and a deep chest and slims down to the hipline.

The expression in your eyes is warm and bright. Basically you are a generous person. You have a regal bearing and your walk is almost catlike. You have very straight posture and will probably experience some back problem during your lifetime.

You wear your hair in a style which falls down upon your forehead. A lion's mane will fall upon his face and the Leo Ascendant person's hair will fall upon his or her face in some manner. Men with a Leo Ascendant tend to lose their hair as they mature and will often grow a beard or mustache.

You have a pleasant voice and a beautiful smile. Your whole face lights up when you smile. When in a sombre mood, the corners of your mouth turn down. Your upper lip is quite thin and your lower lip is full and protrudes slightly. Your ears are regular to large in size with long earlobes. Quite often Leo Ascendant individuals will have a snub nose like that of a lion and the nostrils may be large.

You are charming and diplomatic. You are adept at counselling others and assisting them in making the right decision but have difficulty in making a decision on your own behalf. You will weigh all the pros and cons to a dilemma before reaching a conclusion and can be extremely determined once your mind is set.

You are analytical and detail minded. You will keep books or records in connection with your work and at some time in your life will attain a position of authority. You could have a natural talent for teaching or writing.

You enjoy sports and could successfully compete in sports. You could have a father figure or an older person who will help you in your work. At some point in your career, you will work for the government or for a large corporation.

As you mature, your thinking will change in connection with one of your parents. You may have thought that one of your parents was too dictatorial or too controlling. You may even have felt unloved by one of your parents. Whatever thoughts you have about a parent will completely change as you age.

You become emotionally upset when involved with family problems. You could have an allergic reaction to a certain type of food.

You may feel strongly religious at some point in your life or it could be that you will completely change your feelings about religion during your lifetime.

You have two entirely different groups of friends, each group representing a different area in your life. Your friends will be busy working on projects and you will be actively involved with your friends.

You like to go first class when you travel and may travel to a distant or foreign land. There will come a time when you will move to a completely different location in order to start life anew.

Leo Ascendant/Aries Sun

Your Sun is in the sign of Aries and if you were born within the time frame listed below, your Ascendant sign is Leo.

Date of Birth	Time of Birth
March 21 to March 24	1:10 p.m. to 3:50 p.m.
March 25 to March 29	1:00 p.m. to 3:20 p.m.
March 30 to April 3	12:50 p.m. to 3:10 p.m.
April 4 to April 9	12:10 p.m. to 3:00 p.m.
April 10 to April 14	12:00 Noon to 2:20 p.m.
April 15 to April 19	11:50 a.m. to 2:00 p.m.

You will travel to distant and foreign lands. You may live in a land far from your birthplace. You could have a natural talent for teaching or writing. At some time in your life, you will attain a position of authority.

Leo Ascendant/Taurus Sun

Your Sun is in the sign of Taurus and if you were born within the time frame listed below, your Ascendant sign is Leo.

Date of Birth	Time of Birth
April 20 to April 24	11:15 a.m. to 2:00 p.m.
April 25 to April 28	11:00 a.m. to 1:45 p.m.
April 29 to May 3	10:30 a.m. to 1:15 p.m.
May 4 to May 9	10:15 a.m. to 1:00 p.m.
May 10 to May 15	10:00 a.m. to 12:45 p.m.
May 16 to May 20	9:45 a.m. to 12:15 p.m.

The combination of a Leo Ascendant and a Taurus Sun gives you much persistence. You will pursue your goals with steadfast determination. You take pride in your work and at some time in your life will attain a position of authority.

Leo Ascendant/Gemini Sun

Your Sun is in the sign of Gemini and if you were born within the time frame listed below, your Ascendant sign is Leo.

Date of Birth	Time of Birth
May 21 to May 26	9:10 a.m. to 11:50 a.m.
May 27 to May 31	8:30 a.m. to 11:15 a.m.
June 1 to June 5	8:15 a.m. to 11:00 a.m.
June 6 to June 10	8:00 a.m. to 10:40 a.m.
June 11 to June 16	7:50 a.m. to 10:15 a.m.
June 17 to June 21	7:10 a.m. to 10:00 a.m.

Friendships are important to you. You will have one particular friend you will care for very much. You enjoy being with your friends. At some time in your life, you will attain a position of authority.

Leo Ascendant/Cancer Sun

Your Sun is in the sign of Cancer and if you were born within the time frame listed below, your Ascendant sign is Leo.

Date of Birth	Time of Birth
June 22 to June 27	7:10 a.m. to 9:50 a.m.
June 28 to June 30	7:00 a.m. to 9:30 a.m.
July 1 to July 5	6:20 a.m. to 9:10 a.m.
July 6 to July 10	6:15 a.m. to 8:50 a.m.
July 11 to July 16	6:00 a.m. to 8:15 a.m.
July 17 to July 22	5:50 a.m. to 7:55 a.m.

You were shy in your youth. There was some situation which introduced you to sorrow at an early age. Perhaps there was an illness or a separation from someone dear to you which made you feel lonely or unloved. At some time in your life, you will attain a position of authority.

Leo Ascendant/Leo Sun

Your Sun is in the sign of Leo and if you were born within the time frame listed below, your Ascendant sign is also Leo.

Date of Birth	Time of Birth
Jul 23 to July 27	5:10 a.m. to 7:40 a.m.
July 28 to July 31	5:00 a.m. to 7:10 a.m.
August 1 to August 5	4:20 a.m. to 7:00 a.m.
August 6 to August 10	4:10 a.m. to 6:50 a.m.
August 11 to August 16	4:00 a.m. to 6:10 a.m.
August 17 to August 23	3:15 a.m. to 5:50 a.m.

You are the archetype for all Leo Ascendants. Your outline is the Leo Ascendant mold and everyone with the sign of Leo on the Ascendant is cast from this mold. The placement of the planets in a chart has a significant effect upon an individual but if the mold is cast in the form of a Leo, then that is how the child will grow.

Leo Ascendant/Virgo Sun

Your Sun is in the sign of Virgo and if you were born within the time frame listed below, your Ascendant sign is Leo.

Date of Birth	Time of Birth
August 24 to August 28	2:50 a.m. to 5:45 a.m.
August 29 to August 31	2:30 a.m. to 5:10 a.m.
September 1 to September 5	2:20 a.m. to 5:00 a.m.
September 6 to September 10	2:10 a.m. to 4:50 a.m.
September 11 to September 17	2:00 a.m. to 4:20 a.m.
September 18 to September 22	1:50 a.m. to 4:00 a.m.

You are analytical and detail minded in connection with your work. You recognize quality and want the best. At some time in your life, you will be involved in the world of entertainment, fashion or gambling.

Leo Ascendant/Libra Sun

Your Sun is in the sign of Libra and if you were born within the time frame listed below, your Ascendant sign is Leo.

Date of Birth	Time of Birth
September 23 to September 27	1:10 a.m. to 3:50 a.m.
September 28 to September 30	1:00 a.m. to 3:10 a.m.
October 1 to October 5	12:50 a.m. to 3:00 a.m.
October 6 to October 10	12:15 a.m. to 2:50 a.m.
October 11 to October 17	Midnight to 2:20 a.m.
October 18 to October 23	11:30 p.m. to 2:00 a.m.

You have a charming nature and a dislike for boring physical labor. You can be rather particular about your hair and don't like anyone messing with it. You will have a desire to communicate or express yourself in some way. You will travel.

Leo Ascendant/Scorpio Sun

Your Sun is in the sign of Scorpio and if you were born within the time frame listed below, your Ascendant sign is Leo.

Date of Birth	Time of Birth
October 24 to October 28	11:00 p.m. to 1:50 a.m.
October 29 to October 31	10:50 p.m. to 1:10 a.m.
November 1 to November 6	10:20 p.m. to 1:00 a.m.
November 7 to November 12	10:10 p.m. to 12:50 a.m.
November 13 to November 18	9:50 p.m. to 12:10 a.m.
November 19 to November 22	9:20 p.m. to Midnight

You have much pride in your home and want a home you can be proud of. You will prefer to entertain in your home. Your success in life will be more fully realized in your mature years.

Leo Ascendant/Sagittarius Sun

Your Sun is in the sign of Sagittarius and if you were born within the time frame listed below, your Ascendant sign is Leo.

Date of Birth	Time of Birth
November 23 to November 27	9:00 p.m. to 11:50 p.m.
November 28 to December 1	8:50 p.m. to 11:20 p.m.
December 2 to December 6	8:20 p.m. to 11:00 p.m.
December 7 to December 11	8:10 p.m. to 10:50 p.m.
December 12 to December 16	8:00 p.m. to 10:10 p.m.
December 17 to December 21	7:20 p.m. to 10:00 p.m.

You have a natural wit and a genuine dislike for confining situations. You could have an innate talent for teaching or writing and at some point in your life will be involved in the world of entertainment, fashion or gambling.

Leo Ascendant/Capricorn Sun

Your Sun is in the sign of Capricorn and if you were born within the time frame listed below, your Ascendant sign is Leo.

Date of Birth	Time of Birth
December 22 to December 26	7:10 p.m. to 9:50 p.m.
December 27 to December 31	7:00 p.m. to 9:10 p.m.
January 1 to January 4	6:20 p.m. to 9:00 p.m.
January 5 to January 10	6:10 p.m. to 8:50 p.m.
January 11 to January 15	6:00 p.m. to 8:10 p.m.
January 16 to January 19	5:20 p.m. to 8:00 p.m.

Those born with the Sun in Capricorn often appear old when they are young and young when they are old. You may have endured some restriction or responsibility in your young years which prevented a carefree childhood. At some time in your life, you will attain a position of authority through your work.

Leo Ascendant/Aquarius Sun

Your Sun is in the sign of Aquarius and if you were born within the time frame listed below, your Ascendant sign is Leo.

Date of Birth	Time of Birth
January 20 to January 24	5:10 p.m. to 8:00 p.m.
January 25 to January 29	5:00 p.m. to 7:50 p.m.
January 30 to February 2	4:50 p.m. to 7:10 p.m.
February 3 to February 7	4:10 p.m. to 7:00 p.m.
February 8 to February 12	4:00 p.m. to 6:10 p.m.
February 13 to February 18	3:50 p.m. to 6:00 p.m.

You will work with the public. You could work in a partnership. You have a pleasant, agreeable personality but will rebel in no uncertain terms if you feel you are being forced into something against your will.

Leo Ascendant/Pisces Sun

Your Sun is in the sign of Pisces and if you were born within the time frame listed below, your Ascendant sign is Leo.

Date of Birth	Time of Birth
February 19 to February 23	3:10 p.m. to 5:50 p.m.
February 24 to February 27	3:00 p.m. to 5:20 p.m.
February 28 to March 3	2:50 p.m. to 5:10 p.m.
March 4 to March 9	2:20 p.m. to 5:00 p.m.
March 10 to March 14	2:10 p.m. to 4:10 p.m.
March 15 to March 20	2:00 p.m. to 4:00 p.m.

You have a strong interest in the mysteries of life and in the subject of life and the hereafter. You could receive money from the government and/or insurance benefits. There is a possibility you will receive an inheritance.

Chapter VI

The Virgo Ascendant Person

You have a slender physique which is quite well proportioned and you should remain slender throughout your lifetime. If you do gain extra weight, it will first appear in the stomach area. There is often some irregularity in a Virgo Ascendant's otherwise flawless body. This physical flaw is usually slight and could display itself in the form of a turned-in toe.

Those with a Virgo Ascendant are rather fastidious and will not adorn themselves with anything that hints of clutter. You give the appearance of cleanliness and neatness.

Your head is small and your features are small and neat. A Virgo Ascendant person could have a nicely formed nose but sometimes the nose is slightly pointed or hooked. The bridge of the nose is small, giving a narrow space between the eyes. Virgos rarely have eyes that are set wide apart. Your mouth is not too large and your lips are rather thin.

This Ascendant sign offers a neat looking appearance and will not give a fleshy look to any of the features.

You are observant and can be quite discriminating. At a social function or party, you will often prefer to sit and observe, letting others do the entertaining.

You are analytical and detail minded. Once the mind is set, you have great determination. You are adept in dealing with subjects having to do with figures or mathematics and when you take up a subject, you like to learn everything about it.

You can be diplomatic in connection with financial matters but there will come a time when you will have a major disagreement over money.

You dislike confusion in either your thinking or surroundings and will be quite particular about maintaining a clean and uncluttered household. You could live in a distant or foreign land at some time in your life.

When you shop, it is often difficult to decide upon a specific purchase. If you finally do make up your mind about an item, you will usually have it altered or changed in some manner so that it more closely conforms to your wishes.

You seek perfection in whatever you attempt, which can be hard on your nervous system. You have exquisite taste and could have a natural talent for interior decorating or dress designing.

You will have two completely different careers in your lifetime. At some point in your life, you will work in a form of partnership. You will be busy in your work and will expect your co-workers to do their share. In one of your positions, you will have much communication with the public and your work could involve some travel.

During your lifetime, you will either work in the health profession and care for patients in general or take care of someone close to you. You will act as counsel for another in connection with benefits from the government and/or insurance benefits.

In astrology, it is said that Virgos wish to serve. It has also been said that Virgos are the power behind the throne. With your Virgo Ascendant, you will find some area in your life where you can serve as well as control the actions of another. The sign of Virgo rules work and health and therefore this Virgo desire to serve is usually centered in the area of caring for another who is not well.

You will have a friend whom you will consider to be one of your family. You will have a friend who is a good cook. You will meet friends through your work. At some time in your life, you will become very emotional over a friend.

You have much interest in the mysteries of life and in the subject of life and the hereafter.

Virgo Ascendant/Aries Sun

Your Sun is in the sign of Aries and if you were born within the time frame listed below, your Ascendant sign is Virgo.

Date of Birth	Time of Birth
March 21 to March 24	3:50 p.m. to 6:10 p.m.
March 25 to March 29	3:20 p.m. to 6:00 p.m.
March 30 to April 3	3:10 p.m. to 5:50 p.m.
April 4 to April 9	3:00 p.m. to 5:00 p.m.
April 10 to April 14	2:20 p.m. to 4:50 p.m.
April 15 to April 19	2:00 p.m. to 4:20 p.m.

You have a strong interest in the mysteries of life and in the subject of life and the hereafter. You will receive money from the government and/or insurance benefits. There is a possibility you will receive an inheritance.

Virgo Ascendant/Taurus Sun

Your Sun is in the sign of Taurus and if you were born within the time frame listed below, your Ascendant sign is Virgo.

Date of Birth	Time of Birth
April 20 to April 24	2:00 p.m. to 4:00 p.m.
April 25 to April 28	1:45 p.m. to 3:50 p.m.
April 29 to May 3	1:15 p.m. to 3:40 p.m.
May 4 to May 9	1:00 p.m. to 3:10 p.m.
May 10 to May 15	12:45 p.m. to 3:00 p.m.
May 16 to May 20	12:15 p.m. to 2:45 p.m.

At some time in your life, you will live in a distant or foreign land. You could have a natural talent for teaching or writing. You can be very determined in your beliefs.

Virgo Ascendant/Gemini Sun

Your Sun is in the sign of Gemini and if you were born within the time frame listed below, your Ascendant sign is Virgo.

Date of Birth	Time of Birth
May 21 to May 26	11:50 a.m. to 2:10 p.m.
May 27 to May 31	11:15 a.m. to 1:50 p.m.
June 1 to June 5	11:00 a.m. to 1:30 p.m.
June 6 to June 10	10:40 a.m. to 1:00 p.m.
June 11 to June 16	10:15 a.m. to 12:50 p.m.
June 17 to June 21	10:00 a.m. to 12:15 p.m.

You have good organizational ability and take pride in your work. You will have a hobby which could turn into a full time job. At some time in your life, you will live in a distant or foreign land.

Virgo Ascendant/Cancer Sun

Your Sun is in the sign of Cancer and if you were born within the time frame listed below, your Ascendant sign is Virgo.

Date of Birth	Time of Birth
Jun 22 to June 27	9:50 a.m. to 12:00 Noon
Jun 28 to June 30	9:30 a.m. to 11:50 a.m.
July 1 to July 5	9:10 a.m. to 11:20 a.m.
July 6 to July 10	8:50 a.m. to 11:00 a.m.
July 11 to July 16	8:15 a.m. to 10:45 a.m.
July 17 to July 22	7:55 a.m. to 10:20 a.m.

Friendships are important to you. You will have a particular friend with whom you will feel strong emotional ties. You will accept a friend as a member of your own family.

Virgo Ascendant/Leo Sun

Your Sun is in the sign of Leo and if you were born within the time frame listed below, your Ascendant sign is Virgo.

Date of Birth	Time of Birth
July 23 to July 27	7:40 a.m. to 10:00 a.m.
July 28 to July 31	7:10 a.m. to 9:50 a.m.
August 1 to August 5	7:00 a.m. to 9:30 a.m.
August 6 to August 10	6:50 a.m. to 9:00 a.m.
August 11 to August 16	6:10 a.m. to 8:50 a.m.
August 17 to August 23	5:50 a.m. to 8:20 a.m.

You have a smile that lights up your whole face. You were shy in your youth. There was some situation in your formative years which introduced you to sorrow. There could have been an illness or a separation from a loved one which made you feel lonely or unloved at a tender age.

Virgo Ascendant/Virgo Sun

Your Sun is in the sign of Virgo and if you were born within the time frame listed below, your Ascendant sign is also Virgo.

Date of Birth	Time of Birth
August 24 to August 28	5:45 a.m. to 8:00 a.m.
August 29 to August 31	5:10 a.m. to 7:50 a.m.
September 1 to September 5	5:00 a.m. to 7:40 a.m.
September 6 to September 10	4:50 a.m. to 7:00 a.m.
September 11 to September 17	4:20 a.m. to 6:40 a.m.
September 18 to September 22	4:00 a.m. to 6:20 a.m.

You are the archetype for all Virgo Ascendants. Your outline is the Virgo Ascendant mold and everyone with the sign of Virgo on the Ascendant is cast from this mold. The placement of the planets in a chart has a significant effect upon an individual but if the mold is cast in the form of a Virgo, then that is how the child will grow.

Virgo Ascendant/Libra Sun

Your Sun is in the sign of Libra and if you were born within the time frame listed below, your Ascendant sign is Virgo.

Date of Birth	Time of Birth
September 23 to September 27	3:50 a.m. to 6:00 a.m.
September 28 to September 30	3:10 a.m. to 5:50 a.m.
October 1 to October 5	3:00 a.m. to 5:40 a.m.
October 6 to October 10	2:50 a.m. to 5:00 a.m.
October 11 to October 17	2:20 a.m. to 4:50 a.m.
October 18 to October 23	2:00 a.m. to 4:20 a.m.

You recognize quality and want to have the best. You are quite particular about your hair and don't like anyone messing with it. You will either part your hair in the middle or have no definite part at all. At some time in your life, you will be involved in the world of entertainment, fashion or gambling.

Virgo Ascendant/Scorpio Sun

Your Sun is in the sign of Scorpio and if you were born within the time frame listed below, your Ascendant sign is Virgo.

Date of BirthTime of Birth

Date of Birth	Time of Birth
October 24 to October 28	1:50 a.m. to 4:00 a.m.
October 29 to October 31	1:10 a.m. to 3:50 a.m.
November 1 to November 6	1:00 a.m. to 3:30 a.m.
November 7 to November 12	12:50 a.m. to 3:00 a.m.
November 13 to November 18	12:10 a.m. to 2:50 a.m.
November 19 to November 22	Midnight to 2:20 a.m.

You enjoy a good mystery and when you study a subject, you learn everything you can about it. You are determined once your mind is set but there will come a time in your life when you will completely change your thinking in some way.

Virgo Ascendant/Sagittarius Sun

Your Sun is in the sign of Sagittarius and if you were born within the time frame listed below, your Ascendant sign is Virgo.

Date of Birth	Time of Birth
November 23 to November 27	11:50 p.m. to 2:00 a.m.
November 28 to December 1	11:20 p.m. to 1:50 a.m.
December 2 to December 6	11:00 p.m. to 1:20 a.m.
December 7 to December 11	10:50 p.m. to 1:00 a.m.
December 12 to December 16	10:10 p.m. to 12:50 a.m.
December 17 to December 21	10:00 p.m. to 12:20 a.m.

You want a home you can be proud of and at some time in your life will make your home in a distant or foreign land. Your success will be more fully realized in your mature years.

Virgo Ascendant/Capricorn Sun

Your Sun is in the sign of Capricorn and if you were born within the time frame listed below, your Ascendant sign is Virgo.

Date of Birth	Time of Birth
December 22 to December 26	9:50 p.m. to Midnight
December 27 to December 31	9:10 p.m. to 11:50 p.m.
January 1 to January 4	9:00 p.m. to 11:20 p.m.
January 5 to January 10	8:50 p.m. to 11:00 p.m.
January 11 to January 15	8:10 p.m. to 10:50 p.m.
January 16 to January 19	8:00 p.m. to 10:20 p.m.

Those born with the Sun in Capricorn often appear old when they are young and young when they are old. You may have endured some restriction or responsibility in your formative years which prevented a carefree childhood. At some time in your life, you will be involved in the world of entertainment, fashion or gambling.

Virgo Ascendant/Aquarius Sun

Your Sun is in the sign of Aquarius and if you were born within the time frame listed below, your Ascendant sign is Virgo.

Date of Birth	Time of Birth
January 20 to January 24	8:00 p.m. to 10:00 p.m.
January 25 to January 29	7:50 p.m. to 9:50 p.m.
January 30 to February 2	7:10 p.m. to 9:20 p.m.
February 3 to February 7	7:00 p.m. to 9:10 p.m.
February 8 to February 12	6:10 p.m. to 9:00 p.m.
February 13 to February 18	6:00 p.m. to 8:50 p.m.

You take pride in your work. You are analytical and detail minded in connection with your work. You have a friendly, agreeable disposition but you will rebel in no uncertain terms if you feel you are being forced into something against your will.

Virgo Ascendant/Pisces Sun

Your Sun is in the sign of Pisces and if you were born within the time frame listed below, your Ascendant sign is Virgo.

Date of Birth	Time of Birth
February 19 to February 23	5:50 p.m. to 8:10 p.m.
February 24 to February 27	5:20 p.m. to 8:00 p.m.
February 28 to March 3	5:10 p.m. to 7:50 p.m.
March 4 to March 9	5:00 p.m. to 7:10 p.m.
March 10 to March 14	4:10 p.m. to 7:00 p.m.
March 15 to March 20	4:00 p.m. to 6:20 p.m.

You will work with the public. Your sensitive nature gives you an understanding into the behaviour of people. You can be very diplomatic in handling the public. At some time in your life, you will work in a form of partnership.

Chapter VII

The Libra Ascendant Person

The sign of Libra on your Ascendant gives charm and grace. You have an attractive physical appearance and a gracious manner. Your whole demeanor is pleasant and charming. You have a well proportioned body and could be quite slim in your youth. You will gain weight with age but with reasonable care should be able to maintain a neat form.

You are even tempered and easy to get along with. You have a pleasing presence. Your features are well balanced. Your arms and legs are nicely shaped and your wrists and ankles are slim. You have a nice mouth with soft lips and well shaped teeth. You give the appearance of refinement.

You wear your hair in a style with a part in the middle or with no definite part at all. You really dislike anyone messing with your hair.

You have a bright mind and can be quite philosophical. You pick up knowledge with little effort and become bored and restless very easily.

With Libra's well known propensity for balance, you have difficulty making up your mind because you seek balance in your decisions. You will always consider more than one point of view or more than one angle to a situation. However, once your mind is made up, you can be very determined.

You have an appreciation for beauty and could be artistic. You are intuitive and can be strongly affected by your environment. You don't like being delayed over tedious details but will gladly take all the time necessary to acquire details of a mysterious or hidden nature.

You can be diplomatic in your dealings with people and enjoy working with the public. You have the ability to make others feel at ease. In your discussions with people, you try to see their point of view and are thoughtful of their feelings.

You will be as diplomatic as possible in order to keep the peace. You dislike quarrels and disagreements but you do have a temper and are fully capable of making your point known if your courteous manner is misinterpreted.

You probably felt quite restricted in your youth and undoubtedly were impatient to mature. Your family could have a strong influence on your choice of career. At some time in your life, you will work with your family or with a member of your family.

Your work will involve the general public in some way. You will excel in work dealing with the public. There is a strong likelihood that you will form a partnership with a friend.

It is important that your work be interesting. You will actively avoid boring physical labor. You do enjoy sports and could have a natural talent for teaching or writing.

You could receive money from the government and/or insurance benefits. There is a possibility you will receive an inheritance. You will find that your energy comes in waves or surges. It is as though you get a thunderbolt of energy and will work almost non-stop on the project at hand but then you need your relaxation. It is important that you get your rest. Your whole life seems to be an exercise in a balance act. You will overwork and then come to a complete rest.

You really enjoy relaxing but do not like to relax alone. You want someone to be with, to live with and relax with. Although quite independent, you do not like to live alone. You need peace and harmony in your life to keep your system in proper balance.

You will travel extensively during your lifetime. You will travel to distant lands and faraway places.

Libra Ascendant/Aries Sun

Your Sun is in the sign of Aries and if you were born within the time frame listed below, your Ascendant sign is Libra.

Date of Birth	Time of Birth
March 21 to March 24	6:10 p.m. to 9:00 p.m.
March 25 to March 29	6:00 p.m. to 8:50 p.m.
March 30 to April 3	5:50 p.m. to 8:10 p.m.
April 4 to April 9	5:00 p.m. to 7:50 p.m.
April 10 to April 14	4:50 p.m. to 7:10 p.m.
Apr 15 to Apr 19	4:20 p.m. to 7:00 p.m.

Your Libra Ascendant lends charm and diplomacy to your fast paced Aries Sun giving you skill in handling people. You will work with the public and will find success in working with people.

Libra Ascendant/Taurus Sun

Your Sun is in the sign of Taurus and if you were born within the time frame listed below, your Ascendant sign is Libra.

Date of Birth	Time of Birth
April 20 to April 24	4:00 p.m. to 6:45 p.m.
April 25 to April 28	3:50 p.m. to 6:15 p.m.
April 29 to May 3	3:40 p.m. to 6:00 p.m.
May 4 to May 9	3:10 p.m. to 5:30 p.m.
May 10 to May 15	3:00 p.m. to 5:15 p.m.
May 16 to May 20	2:45 p.m. to 5:00 p.m.

You have a strong interest in the mysteries of life and in the subject of life and the hereafter. You could receive money from the government and/or insurance benefits. There is a possibility you will receive an inheritance.

Libra Ascendant/Gemini Sun

Your Sun is in the sign of Gemini and if you were born within the time frame listed below, your Ascendant sign is Libra.

Date of Birth	Time of Birth
May 21 to May 26	2:10 p.m. to 4:15 p.m.
May 27 to May 31	1:50 p.m. to 4:00 p.m.
Jun 1 to June 5	1:30 p.m. to 3:50 p.m.
Jun 6 to June 10	1:00 p.m. to 3:30 p.m.
Jun 11 to June 16	12:50 p.m. to 3:00 p.m.
Jun 17 to June 21	12:15 p.m. to 2:50 p.m.

You will travel and at some time in your life, you will live in a distant or foreign land. You could have a natural talent for teaching or writing.

Libra Ascendant/Cancer Sun

Your Sun is in the sign of Cancer and if you were born within the time frame listed below, your Ascendant sign is Libra.

Date of Birth	Time of Birth
June 22 to June 27	12:00 Noon to 2:20 p.m.
June 28 to June 30	11:50 a.m. to 2:10 p.m.
July 1 to July 5	11:20 a.m. to 2:00 p.m.
July 6 to July 10	11:00 a.m. to 1:30 p.m.
July 11 to July 16	10:45 a.m. to 1:00 p.m.
Jul 17 to Jul 22	10:20 a.m. to 12:45 p.m.

You take pride in your work. You bring a sensitive understanding to your work and to the people you work with. At some time in your life, you will attain a position of authority.

Libra Ascendant/Leo Sun

Your Sun is in the sign of Leo and if you were born within the time frame listed below, your Ascendant sign is Libra.

Date of Birth	Time of Birth
July 23 to July 27	10:00 a.m. to 12:15 p.m.
July 28 to July 31	9:50 a.m. to 12:00 Noon
August 1 to August 5	9:30 a.m. to 11:50 a.m.
August 6 to August 10	9:00 a.m. to 11:15 a.m.
August 11 to August 16	8:50 a.m. to 11:00 a.m.
August 17 to August 23	8:20 a.m. to 10:40 a.m.

Friendships are important to you. Your friends tend to be very determined individuals. You will have a particular friend you will care for very much. At some time in your life, you will attain a position of authority.

Libra Ascendant/Virgo Sun

Your Sun is in the sign of Virgo and if you were born within the time frame listed below, your Ascendant sign is Libra.

Date of Birth	Time of Birth
August 24 to August 28	8:00 a.m. to 10:15 a.m.
August 29 to August 31	7:50 a.m. to 10:00 a.m.
September 1 to September 5	7:40 a.m. to 9:50 a.m.
September 6 to September 10	7:00 a.m. to 9:40 a.m.
September 11 to September 17	6:40 a.m. to 9:10 a.m.
September 18 to September 22	6:20 a.m. to 9:00 a.m.

You were shy in your youth. There was some situation which caused unhappiness in your formative years. Perhaps there was an illness or a separation from someone dear to you which made you feel lonely or unloved at a tender age. You have a strong interest in the mysteries of life.

Libra Ascendant/Libra Sun

Your Sun is in the sign of Libra and if you were born within the time frame listed below, your Ascendant sign is also Libra.

Date of Birth	Time of Birth
September 23 to September 27	6:00 a.m. to 8:20 a.m.
September 28 to September 30	5:50 a.m. to 8:10 a.m.
October 1 to October 5	5:40 a.m. to 8:00 a.m.
October 6 to October 10	5:00 a.m. to 7:20 a.m.
October 11 to October 17	4:50 a.m. to 7:10 a.m.
October 18 to October 23	4:20 a.m. to 7:00 a.m.

You are the archetype for all Libra Ascendants. Your outline is the Libra Ascendant mold and everyone with the sign of Libra on the Ascendant is cast from this mold. The placement of the planets in a chart has a significant effect upon an individual but if the mold is cast in the form of a Libra, then that is how the child will grow.

Libra Ascendant/Scorpio Sun

Your Sun is in the sign of Scorpio and if you were born within the time frame listed below, your Ascendant sign is Libra.

Date of Birth	Time of Birth
October 24 to October 28	4:00 a.m. to 6:30 a.m.
October 29 to October 31	3:50 a.m. to 6:10 a.m.
November 1 to November 6	3:30 a.m. to 6:00 a.m.
November 7 to November 12	3:00 a.m. to 5:50 a.m.
November 13 to November 18	2:50 a.m. to 5:10 a.m.
November 19 to November 22	2:20 a.m. to 5:00 a.m.

You have classic taste and recognize good quality. You like to have the best. At some time in your life, you will be involved in the world of entertainment, fashion or gambling.

Libra Ascendant/Sagittarius Sun

Your Sun is in the sign of Sagittarius and if you were born within the time frame listed below, your Ascendant sign is Libra.

Date of Birth	Time of Birth
November 23 to November 27	2:00 a.m. to 4:10 a.m.
November 28 to December 1	1:50 a.m. to 4:00 a.m.
December 2 to December 6	1:20 a.m. to 3:50 a.m.
December 7 to December 11	1:00 a.m. to 3:20 a.m.
December 12 to December 16	12:50 a.m. to 3:10 a.m.
December 17 to December 21	12:20 a.m. to 3:00 a.m.

You could be a good storyteller. You can be very witty. You have a pleasant, agreeable nature but if anyone attempts to force you into something against your will, you will rebel in no uncertain terms.

Libra Ascendant/Capricorn Sun

Your Sun is in the sign of Capricorn and if you were born within the time frame listed below, your Ascendant sign is Libra.

Date of Birth	Time of Birth
December 22 to December 26	Midnight to 2:50 a.m.
December 27 to December 31	11:50 p.m. to 2:00 a.m.
January 1 to January 4	11:20 p.m. to 1:50 a.m.
January 5 to January 10	11:00 p.m. to 1:20 a.m.
January 11 to January 15	10:50 p.m. to 1:00 a.m.
January 16 to January 19	10:20 p.m. to 12:50 a.m.

Those born with the Sun in Capricorn often appear old when they are young and young when they are old. You may have endured some restriction or responsibility in your young years which prevented a carefree childhood. Your success in life will be more fully realized in your mature years.

Libra Ascendant/Aquarius Sun

Your Sun is in the sign of Aquarius and if you were born within the time frame listed below, your Ascendant sign is Libra.

Date of Birth	Time of Birth
January 20 to January 24	10:00 p.m. to 12:30 a.m.
January 25 to January 29	9:50 p.m. to 12:10 a.m.
January 30 to February 2	9:20 p.m. to Midnight
February 3 to February 7	9:10 p.m. to 11:50 p.m.
February 8 to February 12	9:00 p.m. to 11:10 p.m.
February 13 to February 18	8:50 p.m. to 11:00 p.m.

You are quite creative and could have a natural talent for teaching or writing. At some time in your life, you will be involved in the world of entertainment, fashion or gambling.

Libra Ascendant/Pisces Sun

Your Sun is in the sign of Pisces and if you were born within the time frame listed below, your Ascendant sign is Libra.

Date of Birth	Time of Birth
February 19 to February 23	8:10 p.m. to 10:50 p.m.
February 24 to February 27	8:00 p.m. to 10:10 p.m.
February 28 to March 3	7:50 p.m. to 10:00 p.m.
March 4 to March 9	7:10 p.m. to 9:50 p.m.
March 10 to March 14	7:00 p.m. to 9:10 p.m.
March 15 to March 20	6:20 p.m. to 9:00 p.m.

You take pride in your work. You are analytical and detail minded in connection with your work. At some time in your life, you will attain a position of authority.

Chapter VIII

The Scorpio Ascendant Person

You have a strong deep-chested physique and a tendency to gain weight easily. You could maintain a slim form with the proper diet but quite often the Scorpio Ascendant person is a little on the heavy side and could easily become overweight if care is not taken.

You have beautiful eyes and a penetrating gaze which is almost hypnotic. You are an intense individual. Your presence is felt even if you do not utter a word. You are often intuitive and can be psychic to some degree.

You have a strong will and at times are able to control a situation simply by focusing your energy and powerful will in that direction.

A Scorpio Ascendant individual usually has thick hair and in most cases the hair grows lower on the forehead area.

Your nose is prominent and may have a hump. The eyebrows of a person with Scorpio on the Ascendant could have a bushy appearance or they could have a pointed arch. Your ears are small to regular in size.

Your mouth is large and sensual looking with a full lower lip. Your teeth are rather large. Your voice is convincing and persuasive.

You have a distinctive walk which resembles a kind of duck walk with a little swing to the hip. Your toes tend to point outward and your hip-swing can be very subtle and hardly noticeable or it can be quite obvious.

You have a compelling nature and can be very determined. You can also be quite observant.

When you study a subject, you like to learn everything about it. There are times when you can become so sombre over a particular matter that you make yourself depressed. However, most of the time you are simply interesting and may even be rather fascinating to others.

Your home life is unusual in some way. There will be unexpected events or sudden happenings occurring on a seemingly regular basis. There is something constantly going on in your home. You cannot enjoy the luxury of relaxing for any appreciable length of time without something disrupting your calm.

You could consider one of your parents more as a friend than a parent, or it may be that you will have a child who will look upon you as a friend.

Your work is important to you. You have pride in your work and will take specialized courses in connection with your work. You are prone to headaches at work.

You dislike having anyone supervise you. You are quite independent and capable of working on your own without anyone telling you what to do. You have the ability to make quick decisions when necessary.

You will enter into a secret partnership at some time in your life. You will attain a position of authority in your work.

You will meet most of your friends through your work. You will have a friend who will be very detail minded and a friend who will be extremely fussy and particular. You will work with someone who has a mark or scar on the face or head area.

There is a strong possibility you will make your home in a distant or foreign land at some point in your life. It could be that your parents came from a distant or foreign land. You may be named as an executor in a will.

You have a deep interest in the mysteries of life and in the subject of life and the hereafter.

Scorpio Ascendant/Aries Sun

Your Sun is in the sign of Aries and if you were born within the time frame listed below, your Ascendant sign is Scorpio.

Date of Birth	Time of Birth
March 21 to March 24	9:00 p.m. to 11:00 p.m.
March 25 to March 29	8:50 p.m. to 10:50 p.m.
March 30 to April 3	8:10 p.m. to 10:20 p.m.
April 4 to April 9	7:50 p.m. to 10:10 p.m.
April 10 to April 14	7:10 p.m. to 10:00 p.m.
April 15 to April 19	7:00 p.m. to 9:20 p.m.

Your fast paced Aries Sun in combination with your Scorpio Ascendant turns very analytical and detail minded in connection with your work. Most of your energies will be directed toward your work. You will attain a position of authority.

Scorpio Ascendant/Taurus Sun

Your Sun is in the sign of Taurus and if you were born within the time frame listed below, your Ascendant sign is Scorpio.

Date of Birth	Time of Birth
April 20 to April 24	6:45 p.m. to 9:00 p.m.
April 25 to April 28	6:15 p.m. to 8:20 p.m.
April 29 to May 3	6:00 p.m. to 8:00 p.m.
May 4 to May 9	5:30 p.m. to 7:50 p.m.
May 10 to May 15	5:15 p.m. to 7:30 p.m.
May 16 to May 20	5:00 p.m. to 7:00 p.m.

There is a natural sweetness to your smile and you have a charming way with people. You will work with the public. At some time in your life, you will work in a partnership.

Scorpio Ascendant/Gemini Sun

Your Sun is in the sign of Gemini and if you were born within the time frame listed below, your Ascendant sign is Scorpio.

Date of Birth	Time of Birth
May 21 to May 26	4:15 p.m. to 7:00 p.m.
May 27 to May 31	4:00 p.m. to 6:15 p.m.
June 1 to June 5	3:50 p.m. to 6:00 p.m.
June 6 to June 10	3:30 p.m. to 5:50 p.m.
June 11 to June 16	3:00 p.m. to 5:15 p.m.
June 17 to June 21	2:50 p.m. to 5:00 p.m.

You have a strong interest in the mysteries of life and in the subject of life and the hereafter. You could be named as an executor in a will. There is a possibility you will receive an inheritance.

Scorpio Ascendant/Cancer Sun

Your Sun is in the sign of Cancer and if you were born within the time frame listed below, your Ascendant sign is Scorpio.

Date of Birth	Time of Birth
June 22 to June 27	2:20 p.m. to 5:00 p.m.
June 28 to June 30	2:10 p.m. to 4:20 p.m.
July 1 to July 5	2:00 p.m. to 4:10 p.m.
July 6 to July 10	1:30 p.m. to 4:00 p.m.
July 11 to July 16	1:00 p.m. to 3:20 p.m.
Jul 17 to July 22	12:45 p.m. to 3:00 p.m.

At some time in your life you will live in a distant or foreign land. You will develop a rather philosophic outlook on life as a shield against your own sensitivity. You will attain a position of authority.

Scorpio Ascendant/Leo Sun

Your Sun is in the sign of Leo and if you were born within the time frame listed below, your Ascendant sign is Scorpio.

Date of Birth	Time of Birth
July 23 to July 27	12:15 p.m. to 2:30 p.m.
July 28 to July 31	12:00 Noon to 2:20 p.m.
August 1 to August 5	11:50 a.m. to 2:10 p.m.
August 6 to August 10	11:15 a.m. to 2:00 p.m.
August 11 to August 16	11:00 a.m. to 1:20 p.m.
August 17 to August 23	10:40 a.m. to 1:00 p.m.

You have much determination. You take pride in your work and want a position you can be proud of. You could come before the public. You will attain a position of leadership.

Scorpio Ascendant/Virgo Sun

Your Sun is in the sign of Virgo and if you were born within the time frame listed below, your Ascendant sign is Scorpio.

Date of Birth	Time of Birth
August 24 to August 28	10:15 a.m. to 12:50 p.m.
August 29 to August 31	10:00 a.m. to 12:20 p.m.
September 1 to September 5	9:50 a.m. to 12:10 p.m.
September 6 to September 10	9:40 a.m. to 12:00 Noon
September 11 to September 17	9:10 a.m. to 11:30 a.m.
September 18 to September 22	9:00 a.m. to 11:10 a.m.

Friendships are important to you. You will meet most of your friends through your work. You will have one particular friend who will be very meaningful to you. You take pride in your work and at some time in your life will attain a position of authority.

Scorpio Ascendant/Libra Sun

Your Sun is in the sign of Libra and if you were born within the time frame listed below, your Ascendant sign is Scorpio.

Date of Birth	Time of Birth
September 23 to September 27	8:20 a.m. to 10:55 a.m.
September 28 to September 30	8:10 a.m. to 10:15 a.m.
October 1 to October 5	8:00 a.m. to 10:00 a.m.
October 6 to October 10	7:20 a.m. to 9:40 a.m.
October 11 to October 17	7:10 a.m. to 9:15 a.m.
October 18 to October 23	7:00 a.m. to 9:05 a.m.

You have a strong interest in the mysteries of life. You were shy in your youth and a health problem or a separation from someone dear to you may have introduced you to sorrow at a tender age. You are particular about your hair and don't like anyone messing with it.

Scorpio Ascendant/Scorpio Sun

Your Sun is in the sign of Scorpio and if you were born within the time frame listed below, your Ascendant sign is also Scorpio.

Date of Birth	Time of Birth
October 24 to October 28	6:30 a.m. to 9:00 a.m.
October 29 to October 31	6:10 a.m. to 8:15 a.m.
November 1 to November 6	6:00 a.m. to 8:05 a.m.
November 7 to November 12	5:50 a.m. to 7:45 a.m.
November 13 to November 18	5:10 a.m. to 7:20 a.m.
November 19 to November 22	5:00 a.m. to 7:00 a.m.

You are the archetype for all Scorpio Ascendants. Your outline is the Scorpio Ascendant mold and everyone with the sign of Scorpio on the Ascendant is cast from this mold. The placement of the planets in a chart has a significant effect upon an individual but if the mold is cast in the form of a Scorpio, then that is how the child will grow.

Scorpio Ascendant/Sagittarius Sun

Your Sun is in the sign of Sagittarius and if you were born within the time frame listed below, your Ascendant sign is Scorpio.

Date of Birth	Time of Birth
November 23 to November 27	4:10 a.m. to 7:00 a.m.
November 28 to December 1	4:00 a.m. to 6:50 a.m.
December 2 to December 6	3:50 a.m. to 6:10 a.m.
December 7 to December 11	3:20 a.m. to 6:00 a.m.
December 12 to December 16	3:10 a.m. to 5:20 a.m.
December 17 to December 21	3:00 a.m. to 5:10 a.m.

You recognize quality and want to have the best. At some time in your life, you will be involved in and earn an income from the world of entertainment, fashion or gambling. You will travel.

Scorpio Ascendant/Capricorn Sun

Your Sun is in the sign of Capricorn and if you were born within the time frame listed below, your Ascendant sign is Scorpio.

Date of Birth	Time of Birth
December 22 to December 26	2:50 a.m. to 5:00 a.m.
December 27 to December 31	2:00 a.m. to 4:20 a.m.
January 1 to January 4	1:50 a.m. to 4:10 a.m.
January 5 to January 10	1:20 a.m. to 4:00 a.m.
January 11 to January 15	1:00 a.m. to 3:50 a.m.
January 16 to January 19	12:50 a.m. to 3:10 a.m.

Those born with the Sun in Capricorn often appear old when they are young and young when they are old. You may have endured some restriction or responsibility in your young years which prevented a carefree childhood. You will become more carefree as you mature.

Scorpio Ascendant/Aquarius Sun

Your Sun is in the sign of Aquarius and if you were born within the time frame listed below, your Ascendant sign is Scorpio.

Date of Birth	Time of Birth
January 20 to January 24	12:30 a.m. to 3:00 a.m.
January 25 to January 29	12:10 a.m. to 2:50 a.m.
January 30 to February 2	Midnight to 2:15 a.m.
February 3 to February 7	11:50 p.m. to 2:00 a.m.
February 8 to February 12	11:10 p.m. to 1:50 a.m.
February 13 to February 18	11:00 p.m. to 1:10 a.m.

You want a home you can be proud of and will do most of your entertaining in your home. Your home life will be different from the average household. Your success in life will be more fully realized in your mature years.

Scorpio Ascendant/Pisces Sun

Your Sun is in the sign of Pisces and if you were born within the time frame listed below, your Ascendant sign is Scorpio.

Date of Birth	Time of Birth
February 19 to February 23	10:50 p.m. to 1:10 a.m.
February 24 to February 27	10:10 p.m. to 1:00 a.m.
February 28 to March 3	10:00 p.m. to 12:20 a.m.
March 4 to March 9	9:50 p.m. to 12:10 a.m.
March 10 to March 14	9:10 p.m. to Midnight
March 15 to March 20	9:00 p.m. to 11:15 p.m.

You are creative and could have a natural talent for teaching or writing. At some time in your life, you will be involved in the world of entertainment, fashion or gambling.

Chapter IX

The Sagittarius Ascendant Person

You have a clean cut look with bright eyes and an enthusiastic nature. You like to observe people.

Sagittarius Ascendant people usually have teeth that crowd their mouth. Your teeth could be larger than usual or very crowded together so that your top lip appears to protrude slightly.

You have a sensitive throat area and could have an allergy.

You have a slender physique and may gain a little extra weight with age but people with the sign of Sagittarius on the Ascendant usually do not experience serious weight problems.

You have long slim legs and take long strides when you walk. There is a kind of spring to your step. Men with this Ascendant sign sometimes shuffle their feet as they walk. When you are seated, there may be a tendency to turn your toes inward.

You have quite a high forehead and probably favor long hair. Men with this Ascendant sign will have a receding hairline as they age. Very often Sagittarius Ascendant people have ears that point upward and a protruding anti-helix at the tip of the ear.

When in conversation, you are apt to tilt your head to one side. You are a good conversationalist and can be very witty.

Your thinking may be a little unconventional in certain areas. You like things that are different.

Whether you actually participate in a sport or are a spectator, you will be a fan of some sporting activity.

You have a restless nature and dislike being confined. You love being out-of-doors and enjoy a natural environment.

You are a pleasant, agreeable individual and will gladly listen to suggestions from others but will rebel in no uncertain terms if anyone attempts to force you into something against your will. You are determined once your mind is set.

You can be very frugal in money matters. You may have felt financially restricted in your youth but should feel more financially comfortable in your mature years.

You have a sensitivity concerning your younger years. Perhaps there was an illness in your family. There was some situation which brought a feeling of sorrow to you in your youth.

You will work for a large corporation or for the government. At some point in your career, an older person will help you. You could have a natural talent for teaching or writing. In some way your work will involve money from the general public. It is important that you have a harmonious environment in which to work.

You will have a friend who is considered quite attractive. You will have a friend who is very charming and diplomatic. You will travel with a friend.

You will travel to faraway places. There is a possibility you will receive an inheritance.

Sagittarius Ascendant/Aries Sun

Your Sun is in the sign of Aries and if you were born within the time frame listed below, your Ascendant sign is Sagittarius.

Date of Birth	Time of Birth
March 21 to March 24	11:00 p.m. to 1:10 a.m.
March 25 to March 29	10:50 p.m. to 1:00 a.m.
March 30 to April 3	10:20 p.m. to 12:50 a.m.
April 4 to April 9	10:10 p.m. to 12:20 a.m.
April 10 to April 14	10:00 p.m. to Midnight
April 15 to April 19	9:20 p.m. to 11:20 p.m.

You can be very creative. You can also be very determined once your mind is set. At some time in your life, you will be involved in the world of entertainment, fashion or gambling.

Sagittarius Ascendant/Taurus Sun

Your Sun is in the sign of Taurus and if you were born within the time frame listed below, your Ascendant sign is Sagittarius.

Date of Birth	Time of Birth
Apr 20 to April 24	9:00 p.m. to 10:45 p.m.
April 25 to April 28	8:20 p.m. to 10:30 p.m.
April 29 to May 3	8:00 p.m. to 10:10 p.m.
May 4 to May 9	7:50 p.m. to 10:00 p.m.
May 10 to May 15	7:30 p.m. to 9:45 p.m.
May 16 to May 20	7:00 p.m. to 9:10 p.m.

You take pride in your work. You are analytical and detail minded in connection with your work. At some time in your life, you will attain a position of authority.

Sagittarius Ascendant/Gemini Sun

Your Sun is in the sign of Gemini and if you were born within the time frame listed below, your Ascendant sign is Sagittarius.

Date of Birth	Time of Birth
May 21 to May 26	7:00 p.m. to 9:10 p.m.
May 27 to May 31	6:15 p.m. to 9:00 p.m.
June 1 to June 5	6:00 p.m. to 8:45 p.m.
June 6 to June 10	5:50 p.m. to 8:15 p.m.
June 11 to June 16	5:15 p.m. to 8:00 p.m.
June 17 to June 21	5:00 p.m. to 7:15 p.m.

You will work with the public. You have a knack for handling people and enjoy working with others. At some time in your life, you will work in a partnership.

Sagittarius Ascendant/Cancer Sun

Your Sun is in the sign of Cancer and if you were born within the time frame listed below, your Ascendant sign is Sagittarius.

Date of Birth	Time of Birth
Jun 22 to June 27	5:00 p.m. to 7:10 p.m.
Jun 28 to June 30	4:20 p.m. to 7:00 p.m.
July 1 to July 5	4:10 p.m. to 6:30 p.m.
July 6 to July 10	4:00 p.m. to 6:10 p.m.
July 11 to July 16	3:20 p.m. to 6:00 p.m.
Jul 17 to Jul 22	3:00 p.m. to 5:15 p.m.

You have a deep sensitivity and a strong interest in the mysteries of life and in the subject of life and the hereafter. There is a possibility you will receive an inheritance.

Sagittarius Ascendant/Leo Sun

Your Sun is in the sign of Leo and if you were born within the time frame listed below, your Ascendant sign is Sagittarius.

Date of Birth	Time of Birth
July 23 to July 27	2:30 p.m. to 5:00 p.m.
July 28 to July 31	2:20 p.m. to 4:20 p.m.
August 1 to August 5	2:10 p.m. to 4:10 p.m.
August 6 to August 10	2:00 p.m. to 4:00 p.m.
August 11 to August 16	1:20 p.m. to 3:50 p.m.
August 17 to August 23	1:00 p.m. to 3:10 p.m.

You have a smile that lights up your whole face. You will live in a distant or foreign land at some time in your life. You have much determination and will attain a position of authority.

Sagittarius Ascendant/Virgo Sun

Your Sun is in the sign of Virgo and if you were born within the time frame listed below, your Ascendant sign is Sagittarius.

Date of BirthTime of Birth

August 24 to August 28	12:50 p.m. to 3:00 p.m.
August 29 to August 31	12:20 p.m. to 2:40 p.m.
September 1 to September 5	12:10 p.m. to 2:20 p.m.
September 6 to September 10	12:00 Noon to 2:10 p.m.
September 11 to September 17	11:30 a.m. to 2:00 p.m.
September 18 to September 22	11:10 a.m. to 1:20 p.m.

You take pride in your work. You have an analytical mind and good organizational ability. You can be detail minded in connection with your work and at some time in your life will attain a position of authority.

Sagittarius Ascendant/Libra Sun

Your Sun is in the sign of Libra and if you were born within the time frame listed below, your Ascendant sign is Sagittarius.

Date of Birth	Time of Birth
September 23 to September 27	10:55 a.m. to 1:00 p.m.
September 28 to September 30	10:15 a.m. to 12:50 p.m.
October 1 to October 5	10:00 a.m. to 12:20 p.m.
October 6 to October 10	9:40 a.m. to 12:10 p.m.
October 11 to October 17	9:15 a.m. to 12:00 Noon
Oct 18 to October 23	9:05 a.m. to 11:50 a.m.

You can be charming and quite witty. Friendships are important to you and others feel at ease in your presence. You will have one particular friend who will be very meaningful to you. You are rather fussy about your hair and don't like anyone messing with it.

Sagittarius Ascendant/Scorpio Sun

Your Sun is in the sign of Scorpio and if you were born within the time frame listed below, your Ascendant sign is Sagittarius.

Date of Birth	Time of Birth
October 24 to October 28	9:00 a.m. to 11:10 a.m.
October 29 to October 31	8:15 a.m. to 11:00 a.m.
November 1 to November 6	8:05 a.m. to 10:50 a.m.
November 7 to November 12	7:45 a.m. to 10:20 a.m.
November 13 to November 18	7:20 a.m. to 10:00 a.m.
November 19 to November 22	7:00 a.m. to 9:20 a.m.

You were shy in your youth. There was some situation that caused unhappiness in your young years. Perhaps there was an illness or a separation from someone dear to you which made you feel lonely or unloved at a tender age. You have a strong interest in the mysteries of life.

Sagittarius Ascendant/Sagittarius Sun

Your Sun is in the sign of Sagittarius and if you were born within the time frame listed below, your Ascendant sign is also Sagittarius.

Date of Birth	Time of Birth
November 23 to November 27	7:00 a.m. to 9:10 a.m.
November 28 to December 1	6:50 a.m. to 8:50 a.m.
December 2 to December 6	6:10 a.m. to 8:10 a.m.
December 7 to December 11	6:00 a.m. to 8:00 a.m.
December 12 to December 16	5:20 a.m. to 7:50 a.m.
December 17 to December 21	5:10 a.m. to 7:15 a.m.

You are the archetype for all Sagittarius Ascendants. Your outline is the Sagittarius Ascendant mold and everyone with the sign of Sagittarius on the Ascendant is cast from this mold. The placement of the planets in a chart has a significant effect upon an individual but if the mold is cast in the form of a Sagittarius, then that is how the child will grow.

Sagittarius Ascendant/Capricorn Sun

Your Sun is in the sign of Capricorn and if you were born within the time frame listed below, your Ascendant sign is Sagittarius.

Date of Birth	Time of Birth
December 22 to December 26	5:00 a.m. to 7:10 a.m.
December 27 to December 31	4:20 a.m. to 7:00 a.m.
January 1 to January 4	4:10 a.m. to 6:50 a.m.
January 5 to January 10	4:00 a.m. to 6:10 a.m.
January 11 to January 15	3:50 a.m. to 6:00 a.m.
January 16 to January 19	3:10 a.m. to 5:20 a.m.

Those born with the Sun in Capricorn often appear old when they are young and young when they are old. You may have endured some restriction or responsibility in your young years which prevented a carefree childhood. At some time in your life, you will be involved in the world of entertainment, fashion or gambling. You recognize quality and want to have the best.

Sagittarius Ascendant/Aquarius Sun

Your Sun is in the sign of Aquarius and if you were born within the time frame listed below, your Ascendant sign is Sagittarius.

Date of Birth	Time of Birth
January 20 to January 24	3:00 a.m. to 5:20 a.m.
January 25 to January 29	2:50 a.m. to 5:10 a.m.
January 30 to February 2	2:15 a.m. to 5:00 a.m.
February 3 to February 7	2:00 a.m. to 4:20 a.m.
February 8 to February 12	1:50 a.m. to 4:10 a.m.
February 13 to February 18	1:10 a.m. to 4:00 a.m.

Communication is important to you and you will want to express yourself. Your thinking is advanced in some way. You are a pleasant agreeable individual but will rebel in no uncertain terms if anyone attempts to force you against your will.

Sagittarius Ascendant/Pisces Sun

Your Sun is in the sign of Pisces and if you were born within the time frame listed below, your Ascendant sign is Sagittarius.

Date of Birth	Time of Birth
February 19 to February 23	1:10 a.m. to 3:20 a.m.
February 24 to February 27	1:00 a.m. to 3:10 a.m.
February 28 to March 3	12:20 a.m. to 3:00 a.m.
March 4 to March 9	12:10 a.m. to 2:20 a.m.
March 10 to March 14	Midnight to 2:10 a.m.
March 15 to March 20	11:15 p.m. to 2:00 a.m.

At some time in your life, you will live in a distant or foreign land. You want a home you can be proud of and you want to entertain in your home. Your success in life will be more fully realized in your mature years.

Chapter X

The Capricorn Ascendant Person

You have a slim physique and will remain quite slender throughout your lifetime. You don't appear to have any excess weight. Your skin is drawn tightly over the bony skeleton of your body permitting no flab. It is rare to find an overweight Capricorn Ascendant person. Your legs are slim and you have a rather narrow hipline.

Capricorn Ascendant people have either deep set eyes or fairly large eyes with a slight droop to the eyelids. If one looks deeply into your eyes, a world-weary expression can be detected.

Your neck is slender and your ears lie flat against your head. You have a small mouth with quite thin lips. Your teeth are not too strong and may require frequent attention. Your hair is lank and straight or with little natural curl.

You are conservative and have a very dry sense of humor. You appear rather reserved at times and can be quite discriminating. You have excellent organizational ability and are astute in detecting deception.

You may have felt restricted in your youth. Perhaps there was an illness or possibly some responsibility was thrust upon you in your early years which prevented you from fully enjoying your youth. Those born with their Ascendant in the sign of Capricorn usually appear old when they are young and young when they are old. You will feel much more carefree in your mature years.

You prefer to live in a neighborhood with lots of trees and plants. Ideally, you would like a nice quiet area with lush greenery.

Ordinarily you are not overly friendly with your neighbors. There will be a time when you will live next door to someone with very poor health.

When stressed, you will want to relax in a natural environment amidst trees and plants. If unable to get away to relax, you will sleep much more than usual.

Your home life could be rather hectic and you may work from your home. You will have the latest equipment in your home and will probably be the head of your household.

You could receive your main source of income in a somewhat different manner than a regular paycheck. You could work a couple of different jobs. You are capable of working on a number of projects at the same time.

There is a possibility you will receive an inheritance.

You will work in a partnership at some time in your career. You perform at your best when working in a close harmonious association with another. You have ambition and the perseverance to succeed.

You could work in a distant or foreign land. You will travel in connection with your work and also in connection with your health. At some time in your life, there will be a secret involved with your travel.

You could have a natural talent for teaching or writing. You will have a creative hobby or avocation which will provide much enjoyment and from which you could make money.

You will have a friend who is secretive and a friend who is extremely stubborn. You will have a friend who is very meaningful to you. You will have a breakup with a friend which will have a strong effect upon you.

Yours is a nature which grows stronger with age and more attractive through the years.

Capricorn Ascendant/Aries Sun

Your Sun is in the sign of Aries and if you were born within the
time frame listed below, your Ascendant sign is Capricorn.

Date of Birth	Time of Birth
March 21 to March 24	1:10 a.m. to 3:20 a.m.
March 25 to March 29	1:00 a.m. to 3:00 a.m.
March 30 to April 3	12:50 a.m. to 2:20 a.m.
April 4 to April 9	12:20 a.m. to 2:10 a.m.
April 10 to April 14	Midnight to 2:00 a.m.
April 15 to April 19	11:20 p.m. to 1:20 a.m.

You want a home you can be proud of. You will have the latest
equipment in your home and at some time in your life, you will
work from your home. You will be the head of your household.

Capricorn Ascendant/Taurus Sun

Your Sun is in the sign of Taurus and if you were born within the
time frame listed below, your Ascendant sign is Capricorn.

Date of Birth	Time of Birth
April 20 to April 24	10:45 p.m. to 12:45 a.m.
April 25 to April 28	10:30 p.m. to 12:30 a.m.
April 29 to May 3	10:10 p.m. to 12:20 a.m.
May 4 to May 9	10:00 p.m. to Midnight
May 10 to May 15	9:45 p.m. to 11:50 p.m.
May 16 to May 20	9:10 p.m. to 11:10 p.m.

You have a pleasant voice and a natural sweetness to your smile.
At some time in your life, you will be involved in the world of
entertainment, fashion or gambling.

Capricorn Ascendant/Gemini Sun

Your Sun is in the sign of Gemini and if you were born within the time frame listed below, your Ascendant sign is Capricorn.

Date of Birth	Time of Birth
May 21 to May 26	9:10 p.m. to 11:00 p.m.
May 27 to May 31	9:00 p.m. to 10:50 p.m.
June 1 to June 5	8:45 p.m. to 10:30 p.m.
June 6 to June 10	8:15 p.m. to 10:10 p.m.
June 11 to June 16	8:00 p.m. to 10:00 p.m.
June 17 to June 21	7:15 p.m. to 9:15 p.m.

You take pride in your work. You are analytical and detail minded in connection with your work. At some time in your life, you will attain a position of authority.

Capricorn Ascendant/Cancer Sun

Your Sun is in the sign of Cancer and if you were born within the time frame listed below, your Ascendant sign is Capricorn.

Date of Birth	Time of Birth
June 22 to June 27	7:10 p.m. to 9:00 p.m.
June 28 to June 30	7:00 p.m. to 8:45 p.m.
July 1 to July 5	6:30 p.m. to 8:15 p.m.
July 6 to July 10	6:10 p.m. to 8:00 p.m.
July 11 to July 16	6:00 p.m. to 7:45 p.m.
Jul 17 to July 22	5:15 p.m. to 7:15 p.m.

You will work with the public. You have a sensitivity to the needs of the public and a knack for handling people. At some time in your life, you will work in a partnership.

Capricorn Ascendant/Leo Sun

Your Sun is in the sign of Leo and if you were born within the time frame listed below, your Ascendant sign is Capricorn.

Date of Birth	Time of Birth
July 23 to July 27	5:00 p.m. to 7:00 p.m.
July 28 to July 31	4:20 p.m. to 6:45 p.m.
August 1 to August 5	4:10 p.m. to 6:30 p.m.
August 6 to August 10	4:00 p.m. to 6:10 p.m.
August 11 to August 16	3:50 p.m. to 5:45 p.m.
August 17 to August 23	3:10 p.m. to 5:20 p.m.

Your whole face lights up when you smile. You have a strong interest in the mysteries of life and in the subject of life and the hereafter. There is a possibility you will receive an inheritance.

Capricorn Ascendant/Virgo Sun

Your Sun is in the sign of Virgo and if you were born within the time frame listed below, your Ascendant sign is Capricorn.

Date of Birth	Time of Birth
August 24 to August 28	3:00 p.m. to 5:00 p.m.
August 29 to August 31	2:40 p.m. to 4:40 p.m.
September 1 to September 5	2:20 p.m. to 4:20 p.m.
September 6 to September 10	2:10 p.m. to 4:05 p.m.
September 11 to September 17	2:00 p.m. to 3:55 p.m.
September 18 to September 22	1:20 p.m. to 3:15 p.m.

At some time in your life, you will live and work in a distant or foreign land. You are analytical and detail minded in your thinking and could have a natural talent for teaching or writing.

Capricorn Ascendant/Libra Sun

Your Sun is in the sign of Libra and if you were born within the time frame listed below, your Ascendant sign is Capricorn.

Date of Birth	Time of Birth
September 23 to September 27	1:00 p.m. to 3:00 p.m.
September 28 to September 30	12:50 p.m. to 2:50 p.m.
October 1 to October 5	12:20 p.m. to 2:40 p.m.
October 6 to October 10	12:10 p.m. to 2:10 p.m.
October 11 to October 17	12:00 Noon to 2:00 p.m.
October 18 to October 23	11:50 a.m. to 1:30 p.m.

You want a career you can be proud of. You dislike boring physical labor. At some time in your life, you will attain a position of authority. You are particular about your hair and don't like anyone messing with it.

Capricorn Ascendant/Scorpio Sun

Your Sun is in the sign of Scorpio and if you were born within the time frame listed below, your Ascendant sign is Capricorn.

Date of Birth	Time of Birth
October 24 to October 28	11:10 a.m. to 1:10 p.m.
October 29 to October 31	11:00 a.m. to 1:00 p.m.
November 1 to November 6	10:50 a.m. to 12:30 p.m.
November 7 to November 12	10:20 a.m. to 12:10 p.m.
November 13 to November 18	10:00 a.m. to 12:00 Noon
November 19 to November 22	9:20 a.m. to 11:20 a.m.

Friendships are important to you. You have a knack for bringing people together. You will have a friend who is rather secretive and a friend who is quite stubborn. You will have a friend who will be very meaningful to you.

Capricorn Ascendant/Sagittarius Sun

Your Sun is in the sign of Sagittarius and if you were born within the time frame listed below, your Ascendant sign is Capricorn.

Date of Birth	Time of Birth
November 23 to November 27	9:10 a.m. to 11:00 a.m.
November 28 to December 1	8:50 a.m. to 10:50 a.m.
December 2 to December 6	8:10 a.m. to 10:10 a.m.
December 7 to December 11	8:00 a.m. to 10:00 a.m.
December 12 to December 16	7:50 a.m. to 9:50 a.m.
December 17 to December 21	7:15 a.m. to 9:10 a.m.

You were shy in your youth. There was some situation which caused unhappiness in your young years. There could have been a health problem or a separation from someone dear to you which made you feel lonely or unloved at a tender age. You will have a strong interest in the mysteries of life.

Capricorn Ascendant/Capricorn Sun

Your Sun is in the sign of Capricorn and if you were born within the time frame listed below, your Ascendant sign is also Capricorn.

Date of Birth	Time of Birth
December 22 to December 26	7:10 a.m. to 9:10 a.m.
December 27 to December 31	7:00 a.m. to 9:00 a.m.
January 1 to January 4	6:50 a.m. to 8:50 a.m.
January 5 to January 10	6:10 a.m. to 8:10 a.m.
January 11 to January 15	6:00 a.m. to 8:00 a.m.
January 16 to January 19	5:20 a.m. to 7:10 a.m.

You are the archetype for all Capricorn Ascendants. Your outline is the Capricorn Ascendant mold and everyone with the sign of Capricorn on the Ascendant is cast from this mold. The placement of the planets in a chart has a significant effect upon an individual but if the mold is cast in the form of a Capricorn, then that is how the child will grow.

Capricorn Ascendant/Aquarius Sun

Your Sun is in the sign of Aquarius and if you were born within the time frame listed below, your Ascendant sign is Capricorn.

Date of Birth	Time of Birth
January 20 to January 24	5:20 a.m. to 7:10 a.m.
January 25 to January 29	5:10 a.m. to 7:00 a.m.
January 30 to February 2	5:00 a.m. to 6:50 a.m.
February 3 to February 7	4:20 a.m. to 6:20 a.m.
February 8 to February 12	4:10 a.m. to 6:10 a.m.
February 13 to February 18	4:00 a.m. to 5:20 a.m.

You recognize quality and want to have the best. At some time in your life, you will be involved in the world of entertainment, fashion or gambling.

Capricorn Ascendant/Pisces Sun

Your Sun is in the sign of Pisces and if you were born within the time frame listed below, your Ascendant sign is Capricorn.

Date of Birth	Time of Birth
February 19 to February 23	3:20 a.m. to 5:20 a.m.
February 24 to February 27	3:10 a.m. to 5:10 a.m.
February 28 to March 3	3:00 a.m. to 5:00 a.m.
March 4 to March 9	2:20 a.m. to 4:20 a.m.
March 10 to March 14	2:10 a.m. to 4:00 a.m.
March 15 to March 20	2:00 a.m. to 3:50 a.m.

You want to communicate or express yourself in some way. You could have a natural talent for teaching or writing. You have a strong interest in the mysteries of life.

Chapter XI

The Aquarius Ascendant Person

The sign of Aquarius rules freedom and with this sign on your Ascendant, you are a free thinker with an independent nature. You march to the beat of a different drummer.

You are a pleasant, agreeable individual but if anyone attempts to force you against your will, you will rebel in no uncertain terms.

You think your own thoughts but will listen to the ideas of others. Basically, you are a humanitarian and get along with people.

Your physique is firm and deep-chested and your shoulders are square. You have a good firm body in youth but could gain weight easily with age if a proper diet is not maintained.

You seem to have a glint or gleam of laughter in your eyes and a ready smile. When not smiling, you have a tendency to hold your mouth quite compressed. You have a clear loud voice.

Your posture is straight and there is a bounce or spring to your step. Aquarius Ascendant individuals have weak ankles and the calf of the leg is often more highly placed than usual. You could be susceptible to charley horses or cramps in the legs.

You rarely complain but can be very impatient. You are observant and able to pick up knowledge easily and could have a difficult time turning off your mind for it is always racing. You can be quite determined once your mind is set.

When you were a youngster you may have felt your thinking was a little different than your peers. Your thinking is different for it is more advanced in certain areas. You could have a natural talent for teaching.

You can be influenced very much through sympathy. Family problems can be emotionally upsetting, especially matters involving the health of your family. When emotionally upset, your idea of relaxation is a good meal and a relaxing drink. This seems to calm your nervous system.

There may have been a time when you thought one of your parents was too dictatorial. You may have thought this parent was responsible for a family situation which brought unhappiness in your youth. There will come a time when you will completely change your thinking in connection with this parent.

You want to have a nice peaceful home and prefer to stay home and entertain at home rather than go out on the town.

There will be a time in your life when you will have the need to hide your financial records and money from another person.

You will work with the public. You are able to work very well with people and at some time will work with a member of your family. You like to maintain a certain amount of control in your work. At times your work can make you emotionally upset. You will make a major change in your career at some point in your life.

You will travel extensively and do not particularly like to travel alone but you do like to go first class.

You will enjoy the friendship of people from all walks of life and will meet people from foreign countries and distant lands.

You could have an innate talent for writing or sketching or communicating your ideas in some way. You will have a creative hobby or avocation which will provide much enjoyment.

Aquarius Ascendant/Aries Sun

Your Sun is in the sign of Aries and if you were born within the time frame listed below, your Ascendant sign is Aquarius.

Date of Birth	Time of Birth
March 21 to March 24	3:20 a.m. to 5:00 a.m.
March 25 to March 29	3:00 a.m. to 4:50 a.m.
March 30 to April 3	2:20 a.m. to 4:10 a.m.
April 4 to April 9	2:10 a.m. to 4:00 a.m.
April 10 to April 14	2:00 a.m. to 3:20 a.m.
April 15 to Apr 19	1:20 a.m. to 3:00 a.m.

Communication is important to you. You have a quick mind which is always working and you will want to express yourself in some way. You could have a natural talent for teaching or writing.

Aquarius Ascendant/Taurus Sun

Your Sun is in the sign of Taurus and if you were born within the time frame listed below, your Ascendant sign is Aquarius.

Date of Birth	Time of Birth
April 20 to April 24	12:45 a.m. to 2:50 a.m.
April 25 to April 28	12:30 a.m. to 2:30 a.m.
April 29 to May 3	12:20 a.m. to 2:00 a.m.
May 4 to May 9	Midnight to 1:50 a.m.
May 10 to May 15	11:50 p.m. to 1:15 a.m.
May 16 to May 20	11:10 p.m. to 1:00 a.m.

You want a home you can be proud of. You will do most of your entertaining at home and you could be an excellent cook. Your success in life will be more fully realized in your mature years.

Aquarius Ascendant/Gemini Sun

Your Sun is in the sign of Gemini and if you were born within the time frame listed below, your Ascendant sign is Aquarius.

Date of Birth	Time of Birth
May 21 to May 26	11:00 p.m. to 1:00 a.m.
May 27 to May 31	10:50 p.m. to 12:45 a.m.
June 1 to June 5	10:30 p.m. to 12:10 a.m.
June 6 to June 10	10:10 p.m. to 11:50 p.m.
June 11 to June 16	10:00 p.m. to 11:15 p.m.
June 17 to June 21	9:15 p.m. to 11:00 p.m.

You will usually be found working on some project. Even in relaxation, you will work on your projects. At some time in your life, you will be involved in the world of entertainment, fashion or gambling.

Aquarius Ascendant/Cancer Sun

Your Sun is in the sign of Cancer and if you were born within the time frame listed below, your Ascendant sign is Aquarius.

Date of Birth	Time of Birth
June 22 to June 27	9:00 p.m. to 10:50 p.m.
June 28 to June 30	8:45 p.m. to 10:10 p.m.
July 1 to July 5	8:15 p.m. to 10:00 p.m.
July 6 to July 10	8:00 p.m. to 9:50 p.m.
July 11 to July 16	7:45 p.m. to 9:15 p.m.
July 17 to July 22	7:15 p.m. to 9:00 p.m.

You bring a nurturing warmth to your workplace and can be quite analytical and detail minded in connection with your work. You take pride in your work and will attain a position of authority.

Aquarius Ascendant/Leo Sun

Your Sun is in the sign of Leo and if you were born within the time frame listed below, your Ascendant sign is Aquarius.

Date of Birth	Time of Birth
July 23 to July 27	7:00 p.m. to 8:30 p.m.
July 28 to July 31	6:45 p.m. to 8:20 p.m.
August 1 to August 5	6:30 p.m. to 8:10 p.m.
August 6 to August 10	6:10 p.m. to 7:50 p.m.
August 11 to August 16	5:45 p.m. to 7:30 p.m.
August 17 to August 23	5:20 p.m. to 7:00 p.m.

You have a smile that lights up your whole face. You have a charming way with people and will find success through your work with the public. At some time in your life, you will work in a partnership.

Aquarius Ascendant/Virgo Sun

Your Sun is in the sign of Virgo and if you were born within the time frame listed below, your Ascendant sign is Aquarius.

Date of Birth	Time of Birth
August 24 to August 28	5:00 p.m. to 6:40 p.m.
August 29 to August 31	4:40 p.m. to 6:10 p.m.
September 1 to September 5	4:20 p.m. to 6:00 p.m.
September 6 to September 10	4:05 p.m. to 5:50 p.m.
September 11 to September 17	3:55 p.m. to 5:20 p.m.
September 18 to September 22	3:15 p.m. to 5:00 p.m.

You have a strong interest in the mysteries of life and in the subject of life and the hereafter. You could receive money from the government and/or insurance benefits. There is a possibility you will receive an inheritance.

Aquarius Ascendant/Libra Sun

Your Sun is in the sign of Libra and if you were born within the time frame listed below, your Ascendant sign is Aquarius.

Date of Birth	Time of Birth
September 23 to September 27	3:00 p.m. to 4:30 p.m.
September 28 to September 30	2:50 p.m. to 4:15 p.m.
October 1 to October 5	2:40 p.m. to 4:05 p.m.
October 6 to October 10	2:10 p.m. to 3:50 p.m.
October 11 to October 17	2:00 p.m. to 3:20 p.m.
October 18 to October 23	1:30 p.m. to 3:00 p.m.

At some time in your life, you will live and work in a distant or foreign land. You have a strong dislike for boring physical labor so your work must be interesting. You can be quite particular about your hair and don't want anyone messing with it.

Aquarius Ascendant/Scorpio Sun

Your Sun is in the sign of Scorpio and if you were born within the time frame listed below, your Ascendant sign is Aquarius.

Date of Birth	Time of Birth
October 24 to October 28	1:10 p.m. to 2:50 p.m.
October 29 to October 31	1:00 p.m. to 2:10 p.m.
November 1 to November 6	12:30 p.m. to 2:00 p.m.
November 7 to November 12	12:10 p.m. to 1:50 p.m.
November 13 to November 18	12:00 Noon to 1:20 p.m.
November 19 to November 22	11:20 a.m. to 1:10 p.m.

You take pride in your work and want a position you can be proud of. At some time in your life, you will completely change your career. You will attain a position of authority.

Aquarius Ascendant/Sagittarius Sun

Your Sun is in the sign of Sagittarius and if you were born within the time frame listed below, your Ascendant sign is Aquarius.

Date of Birth	Time of Birth
November 23 to November 27	11:00 a.m. to 12:30 p.m.
November 28 to December 1	10:50 a.m. to 12:20 p.m.
December 2 to December 6	10:10 a.m. to 12:00 Noon
December 7 to December 11	10:00 a.m. to 11:50 a.m.
December 12 to December 16	9:50 a.m. to 11:20 a.m.
December 17 to December 21	9:10 a.m. to 11:10 a.m.

Friendships are important to you. You will have friends from distant and foreign lands and from all walks of life. You will have a particular friend who will be very meaningful to you. You will enter a partnership with a friend.

Aquarius Ascendant/Capricorn Sun

Your Sun is in the sign of Capricorn and if you were born within the time frame listed below, your Ascendant sign is Aquarius.

Date of Birth	Time of Birth
December 22 to December 26	9:10 a.m. to 10:50 a.m.
December 27 to December 31	9:00 a.m. to 10:20 a.m.
January 1 to January 4	8:50 a.m. to 10:10 a.m.
January 5 to January 10	8:10 a.m. to 9:50 a.m.
January 11 to January 15	8:00 a.m. to 9:20 a.m.
January 16 to January 19	7:10 a.m. to 9:00 a.m.

You have a strong interest in the mysteries of life. You were shy in your youth. There was some situation which caused unhappiness in your young years. There could have been a health problem or a separation from someone dear to you which made you feel lonely or unloved at a tender age.

Aquarius Ascendant/Aquarius Sun

Your Sun is in the sign of Aquarius and if you were born within the time frame listed below, your Ascendant sign is also Aquarius.

Date of Birth	Time of Birth
January 20 to January 24	7:10 a.m. to 8:50 a.m.
January 25 to January 29	7:00 a.m. to 8:40 a.m.
January 30 to February 2	6:50 a.m. to 8:10 a.m.
February 3 to February 7	6:20 a.m. to 8:00 a.m.
February 8 to February 12	6:10 a.m. to 7:20 a.m.
February 13 to February 18	5:20 a.m. to 7:10 a.m.

You are the archetype for all Aquarius Ascendants. Your outline is the Aquarius Ascendant mold and everyone with the sign of Aquarius on the Ascendant is cast from this mold. The placement of the planets in a chart has a significant effect upon an individual but if the mold is cast in the form of an Aquarius, then that is how the child will grow.

Aquarius Ascendant/Pisces Sun

Your Sun is in the sign of Pisces and if you were born within the time frame listed below, your Ascendant sign is Aquarius.

Date of Birth	Time of Birth
February 19 to February 23	5:20 a.m. to 7:10 a.m.
February 24 to February 27	5:10 a.m. to 6:50 a.m.
February 28 to March 3	5:00 a.m. to 6:20 a.m.
February 4 to March 9	4:20 a.m. to 6:10 a.m.
March 10 to March 14	4:00 a.m. to 5:50 a.m.
March 15 to March 20	3:50 a.m. to 5:10 a.m.

You recognize quality and want to have the best. At some time in your life, you will be involved in the world of entertainment, fashion or gambling.

Chapter XII

The Pisces Ascendant Person

There is a softness to your features. Your skin is fair and your eyes have a soulful look. Often a person with the sign of Pisces on the Ascendant will have dreamy looking eyes and heavy eyelids. Your hair is soft, plentiful and unruly. Your nose may have a small lift so that the nostrils or the nasal septum are visible. The bridge of the nose is high with hardly any indentation where it meets the forehead area.

There are many Pisces Ascendant individuals who possess an attractive neat body and who maintain a trim physique but this sign on a person's Ascendant can also give a fullness to the body with a very wide hip span. This type of Pisces Ascendant person can become exceedingly overweight if there is no regard to maintaining a slimming diet.

Whether you have a trim physique or tend to be overweight, you will have small neat feet and small hands.

Your posture is straight and your walk is a saunter or stroll, although the slimmer type Pisces Ascendant person has a faster paced step.

Your mouth is sensitive and you have a soft deep voice. This sign on the Ascendant can give a voice which is also a trifle shrill or higher pitched at times. When in conversation, you have a habit of folding your arms across your chest as you speak or ponder a point.

You are pleasant and agreeable but if provoked, will take a firm stand and you can be very determined once your mind is set.

You will have more than one way of making money in your lifetime. Your thoughts frequently turn to ways and means in which to increase your income. You want a fast return on your investment and don't like to wait in order to buy what you want. You can be extremely impatient.

You do not like anyone telling you how to spend your money and in some way, you will manage the finances in your household. You are a peace loving individual and do not like arguments but there will come a time when you will have a major argument over money.

You take pride in your work and in the projects you are involved with. You can be friendly and congenial while at work but also very persistent. It is through your work that you will attain a position of authority.

When stressed, you will find relaxation in a natural environment with trees and the song of birds or music. If you are unable to get away to relax, you will sleep much more than usual.

You will have friendships with people who are in responsible positions. You will have friends who are either a number of years older or a number of years younger than you. You will have a particular friend for many many years.

Your home life is busy. There will always be something going on in your household. There may be people coming and going at all hours or you may be working on projects or hobbies at all hours. It could be that you will have two homes or that your home will serve the dual purpose of house and office.

At some point in your life, you will move to a completely new location in order to start anew.

Pisces Ascendant/Aries Sun

Your Sun is in the sign of Aries and if you were born within the time frame listed below, your Ascendant sign is Pisces.

Date of Birth	Time of Birth
March 21 to March 24	5:00 a.m. to 6:10 a.m.
March 25 to March 29	4:50 a.m. to 6:00 a.m.
March 30 to April 3	4:10 a.m. to 5:50 a.m.
April 4 to April 9	4:00 a.m. to 5:00 a.m.
April 10 to April 14	3:20 a.m. to 4:50 a.m.
April 15 to April 19	3:00 a.m. to 4:20 a.m.

You recognize quality and want to have the best. You can be rather impatient and don't like to wait to get what you want. At some time in your life, you will be involved in the world of entertainment, fashion or gambling.

Pisces Ascendant/Taurus Sun

Your Sun is in the sign of Taurus and if you were born within the time frame listed below, your Ascendant sign is Pisces.

Date of Birth	Time of Birth
April 20 to April 24	2:50 a.m. to 4:00 a.m.
April 25 to April 28	2:30 a.m. to 3:50 a.m.
April 29 to May 3	2:00 a.m. to 3:30 a.m.
May 4 to May 9	1:50 a.m. to 3:15 a.m.
May 10 to May 15	1:15 a.m. to 2:50 a.m.
May 16 to May 20	1:00 a.m. to 2:30 a.m.

You have a sweet smile and a sensitivity which belies the incredible determination of your will. You will want to express yourself in some way. You could have a natural talent for teaching or writing. You will travel.

Pisces Ascendant/Gemini Sun

Your Sun is in the sign of Gemini and if you were born within the time frame listed below, your Ascendant sign is Pisces.

Date of Birth	Time of Birth
May 21 to May 26	1:00 a.m. to 2:10 a.m.
May 27 to May 31	12:45 a.m. to 1:50 a.m.
June 1 to June 5	12:10 a.m. to 1:30 a.m.
June 6 to June 10	11:50 p.m. to 1:00 a.m.
June 11 to June 16	11:15 p.m. to 12:45 a.m.
June 17 to June 21	11:00 p.m. to 12:20 a.m.

You want a home you can be proud of and will do most of your entertaining in your home. At some point in your life, you will work from your home. Your success in life will be more fully realized in your mature years.

Pisces Ascendant/Cancer Sun

Your Sun is in the sign of Cancer and if you were born within the time frame listed below, your Ascendant sign is Pisces.

Date of Birth	Time of Birth
Jun 22 to June 27	10:50 p.m. to 12:10 a.m.
Jun 28 to June 30	10:10 p.m. to 11:30 p.m.
July 1 to July 5	10:00 p.m. to 11:15 p.m.
July 6 to July 10	9:50 p.m. to 11:00 p.m.
July 11 to July 16	9:15 p.m. to 10:30 p.m.
July 17 to July 22	9:00 p.m. to 10:10 p.m.

You have a warm sensitive nature and a good imagination. You could be a natural storyteller. At some time in your life, you will be involved in the world of entertainment, fashion or gambling.

Pisces Ascendant/Leo Sun

Your Sun is in the sign of Leo and if you were born within the time frame listed below, your Ascendant sign is Pisces.

Date of Birth	Time of Birth
July 23 to July 27	8:30 p.m. to 9:50 p.m.
July 28 to July 31	8:20 p.m. to 9:30 p.m.
August 1 to August 5	8:10 p.m. to 9:20 p.m.
August 6 to August 10	7:50 p.m. to 9:00 p.m.
August 11 to August 16	7:30 p.m. to 8:45 p.m.
August 17 to August 23	7:00 p.m. to 8:30 p.m.

You take pride in your work and want a position you can be proud of. You are analytical and detail minded in connection with your work. You are determined and will attain a position of authority.

Pisces Ascendant/Virgo Sun

Your Sun is in the sign of Virgo and if you were born within the time frame listed below, your Ascendant sign is Pisces.

Date of Birth	Time of Birth
August 24 to August 28	6:40 p.m. to 7:50 p.m.
August 29 to August 31	6:10 p.m. to 7:30 p.m.
September 1 to September 5	6:00 p.m. to 7:20 p.m.
September 6 to September 10	5:50 p.m. to 7:00 p.m.
September 11 to September 17	5:20 p.m. to 6:40 p.m.
September 18 to September 22	5:00 p.m. to 6:20 p.m.

You have a knack for handling people and will find success in working with the public. You are analytical and detail minded in connection with your work. At some time in your life, you will work in a partnership.

Pisces Ascendant/Libra Sun

Your Sun is in the sign of Libra and if you were born within the time frame listed below, your Ascendant sign is Pisces.

Date of Birth	Time of Birth
September 23 to September 27	4:30 p.m. to 5:50 p.m.
September 28 to September 30	4:15 p.m. to 5:40 p.m.
October 1 to October 5	4:05 p.m. to 5:20 p.m.
October 6 to October 10	3:50 p.m. to 5:00 p.m.
October 11 to October 17	3:20 p.m. to 4:30 p.m.
October 18 to October 23	3:00 p.m. to 4:15 p.m.

You have a strong interest in the mysteries of life and in the secret of life and the hereafter. There is a possibility you will receive an inheritance. You can be particular about your hair and don't like anyone messing with it.

Pisces Ascendant/Scorpio Sun

Your Sun is in the sign of Scorpio and if you were born within the time frame listed below, your Ascendant sign is Pisces.

Date of Birth	Time of Birth
October 24 to October 28	2:50 p.m. to 3:50 p.m.
October 29 to October 31	2:10 p.m. to 3:40 p.m.
November 1 to November 6	2:00 p.m. to 3:20 p.m.
November 7 to November 12	1:50 p.m. to 3:00 p.m.
November 13 to November 18	1:20 p.m. to 2:30 p.m.
November 19 to November 22	1:10 p.m. to 2:10 p.m.

At some time in your life, you will work in a distant or foreign land. You take pride in your work and it is through your work that you will attain a position of authority.

Pisces Ascendant/Sagittarius Sun

Your Sun is in the sign of Sagittarius and if you were born within the time frame listed below, your Ascendant sign is Pisces.

Date of Birth	Time of Birth
November 23 to November 27	12:30 p.m. to 1:50 p.m.
November 28 to December 1	12:20 p.m. to 1:30 p.m.
December 2 to December 6	12:00 Noon to 1:15 p.m.
December 7 to December 11	11:50 a.m. to 1:00 p.m.
December 12 to December 16	11:20 a.m. to 12:40 p.m.
December 17 to December 21	11:10 a.m. to 12:20 p.m.

You take pride in your work and want a position you can be proud of. Your work will introduce you to people from all walks of life and from distant and foreign lands. At some time in your life, you will attain a position of authority.

Pisces Ascendant/Capricorn Sun

Your Sun is in the sign of Capricorn and if you were born within the time frame listed below, your Ascendant sign is Pisces.

Date of Birth	Time of Birth
December 22 to December 26	10:50 am to 12:00 Noon
December 27 to December 31	10:20 am to 11:50 a.m.
January 1 to January 4	10:10 am to 11:20 a.m.
January 5 to January 10	9:50 am to 11:00 a.m.
January 11 to January 15	9:20 am to 10:45 a.m.
January 16 to January 19	9:00 am to 10:15 a.m.

Those born with the Sun in Capricorn often appear old when they are young and young when they are old. You may have endured some restriction or responsibility in your youth which prevented a carefree childhood. Friendships are important to you and you will have a particular friend for many many years.

Pisces Ascendant/Aquarius Sun

Your Sun is in the sign of Aquarius and if you were born within the time frame listed below, your Ascendant sign is Pisces.

Date of Birth	Time of Birth
January 20 to January 24	8:50 am to 10:00 a.m
January 25 to January 29	8:40 am to 9:50 a.m.
January 30 to February 2	8:10 am to 9:20 a.m.
February 3 to February 7	8:00 am to 9:10 a.m.
February 8 to February 12	7:20 am to 9:00 a.m.
February 13 to February 18	7:10 am to 8:50 a.m.

You have a strong interest in the mysteries of life. You were shy in your youth. There was some situation in your formative years which caused unhappiness. Possibly there was an illness or a separation from someone dear to you which made you feel lonely or unloved at a tender age.

Pisces Ascendant/Pisces Sun

Your Sun is in the sign of Pisces and if you were born within the time frame listed below, your Ascendant sign is also Pisces.

Date of Birth	Time of Birth
February 19 to February 23	7:10 am to 8:20 a.m.
February 24 to February 27	6:50 am to 7:50 a.m.
February 28 to March 3	6:20 am to 7:20 a.m.
March 4 to March 9	6:10 am to 7:10 a.m.
March 10 to March 14	5:50 am to 7:00 a.m.
March 15 to March 20	5:10 am to 6:20 a.m.

You are the archetype for all Pisces Ascendants. Your outline is the Pisces Ascendant mold and everyone with the sign of Pisces on the Ascendant is cast from this mold. The placement of the planets in a chart has a significant effect upon an individual but if the mold is cast in the form of a Pisces, then that is how the child will grow.